ON MY OWN

Sally Hobart Alexander

ON MY OWN
THE JOURNEY CONTINUES

Farrar Straus Giroux
New York

A C K N O W L E D G M E N T

Many thanks to Dr. Richard Welsh and the excellent staff at the Greater Pittsburgh Guild for the Blind, and to Dr. Robert Wittig

Library of Congress Cataloging-in-Publication Data
Alexander, Sally Hobart.
    On my own : the journey continues / Sally Hobart Alexander. — 1st ed.
    p.   cm.
    The second part of the author's autobiography, of which the first part,
Taking hold, was published in 1994.
    Summary: The author describes the difficulties and accomplishments she
experiences as she adjusts to living independently after losing her sight.
    ISBN 0-374-35641-6
    1. Alexander, Sally Hobart—Juvenile literature. 2. Blind—United
States—Biography—Juvenile literature. [1. Alexander, Sally Hobart.
2. Blind. 3. Physically handicapped. 4. Women—Biography.] I. Title.
HV1792.A44A3   1997
362.4'1'092—dc20   96-36277
[B]

*To Sherry Broad Feldstein and,
again, to Ruth and Fred Alexander,
with love and gratitude*

Part One

❧ 1 ☙

September 1969

I heard a sound, and my heart leaped against my ribs. What could it be? I rushed to the window, held my breath, strained my ears. Cars roared along Bigelow Boulevard; buses and trucks ground up Centre Avenue.

But I had heard a different noise, the clink of metal on brick. And I had to face a terrifying possibility: An intruder, maybe a murderer, was scaling the apartment building toward my window. Any minute, he would rip through the screen.

Despite the September heat, I slammed the window shut. I walked away, then returned, tripping on the corner of the coffee table. *Clunk.* The window lock snapped like a jail cell door. And this sound scared me even more.

What was the matter with me? I'd been fine in this apartment last night—my first night. But my parents had been here to keep me safe. Soon after they left, I began imagining dangers inside and outside the building.

That they had both broken into tears saying goodbye hadn't helped. Daddy was always a blubberer, tearing up at every separation. But when Mom, the rock, began to cry, I decided I was in great peril. I sighed, remembering.

I clicked on another lamp and brushed the TV. If I turned on the television full blast, I'd have company, maybe scare off the intruder.

A floorboard creaked under my foot, throwing my heart into more rapid hammering. Oh, what *was* I doing here? In Pittsburgh. Alone. Would people in the city hurry to my rescue, as they would have back in Conyngham, my small Pennsylvania hometown? There I knew everyone; here I didn't know a soul— at least not in the building. The one man I'd spoken to seemed elderly and deaf, incapable of protecting me even if he heard my screams.

"Terrific!" I muttered, then spoke louder. "Calm down, Sally. This is the top floor." A murderer would break into a first-floor apartment, surely.

I listened to the melodramatic dialogue on the TV and sank onto my bed. Melodramatic, that was how I was acting. I massaged my neck, prickling with per-spiration. This was ridiculous. I'd adjusted to new places before—dormitories at Bucknell, where I'd gone to school, and three apartments in Long Beach, California, where I'd lived most recently. True, they hadn't been in the city, but there was another, bigger difference. Back then, I could see. With one glance out the window I could have assured myself that nobody was scaling the wall.

Now I was blind. Blind, except for seeing light and dark, and a tiny bit of sight out of the lower quarter of my left eye.

A door slammed across the hall, and I jumped as if hearing a gunshot. I hugged myself, feeling the dampness between my shirt and stomach. The heat in the room, the walls bore in on me. Slowly I began to rock.

Oh, no! Rocking! One of the bizarre behaviors of the blind. Providing stimulation. Comfort. I was regressing. In another minute I would be in a fetal position.

I stood and stepped cautiously around unpacked boxes to the door. I listened. My neighbor across the hall played a Paul Simon record. Maybe he was young, like me. I should sashay right over there and knock on the door. "Hi," I'd say. "I came for a visit. Will you guide me to a chair?"

Meeting people was so difficult now. I shuddered. The Paul Simon fan could turn out to be the murderer!

"Stop it," I said, steadying myself against the wall. The blindness made such a big difference. I pressed my hand against my mouth.

Above the blare of the television, another sound caught my ears—a low, rumbling groan. I swung around and tensed. But the groan came from me.

"I am losing my mind," I whispered.

I walked over to my bed and pulled a heavy ceramic vase from the shelf above it. A weapon. I wouldn't succumb without a fight!

One moment I'd convinced myself that there was no murderer. In the next I braced myself for a violent death.

I stretched out on the bed with the vase. Truth was, there already had been a death—to my sight; to my sighted self. The blindness had changed my whole way of life. And now I was on my own, back in the real world again. What had possessed me to think that reentry would be easy?

I had to find a life here, a home, a meaningful job that would support me, good friends, maybe even a boyfriend. Not much to ask for! But I *had* to achieve some of those goals. Otherwise, I'd be thrown back to Conyngham, dependent on my parents. And when they grew old and infirm, I'd become an albatross around the neck of my brother, Bobby, and his wife, Barb, or my sister, Marti, and her husband, Larry. Lovely. And where would Marti put me with three young kids of her own? Tracy was nine, Erik six, and Amy only five.

No, I wouldn't inflict myself on them. I would make it alone, despite the difficulty. And here I was, failing at the very first step. I'd found a place to live, but it felt more like a prison tower than a home.

I pulled the vase closer. The room was stifling with the window closed. But I lay there all night, amid the lit lamps and blaring TV. I lay in bed, gripping my vase, tossing, sleepless, ridiculous with fear.

~ 2 ~

Finally, the sun slanted into the apartment and warmed my cheeks. I opened my eyes. The brightness stung, making me blink. But I was grateful for the vision—any amount of vision.

I put the vase back on the shelf, stood, and pushed up the window. Fresh, moist air slipped around me like a hug. On stiff legs I followed the dark line between my two Navajo rugs, my path to the bathroom. I unlocked the window there, too. I stuck my face, then my entire head under the cold water tap, shocking my body into alertness.

In the kitchen, I touched the metal rim of the gas burner, placed the kettle on top of it, and turned the knob. My movements were as mechanical as a robot's. Simultaneously, I saw the orange-yellow glow and felt the heat. I pulled out milk and a glass, stuck my finger over the rim, and poured. Improper technique, but I was too tired to judge by weight and sound. I drank.

The kettle whistled, and I poured tea. "Ouch!" The boiling water burned my finger. "That'll teach you," I scolded myself.

I slid my feet along the rugs, switching off each lamp and the religious program on the TV. Then I settled back on the bed, propping myself with pillows, sipping the tea.

Already horns blasted, brakes screeched, and the city sounds reached a crescendo. I should forget the rhythmic slapping of the sea on the beach near my California apartment, forget the songs of birds around my parents' home. I needed to develop a taste for this city music.

I shook the webs from my brain and remembered. Five weeks ago, when I'd graduated from the Greater Pittsburgh Guild for the Blind, I'd expected to celebrate the move to this apartment. Yesterday marked a big triumph: being able to live alone again. But instead of celebrating, I'd panicked.

Well, enough of that. Tomorrow I would start my teaching job at the guild, another triumph, and I had to prepare. Training the newly blind wasn't the job of my dreams, but it would keep me from the no-man's-land of poverty until I could afford graduate school and start a new career. Much as I wanted to, I knew I would never teach third grade again.

I touched my churning forehead with the warm mug. I had to make it on my own, as I had after college four years before.

My parents had urged me to stay with them. "We've found you a job," Mom argued, "and there are many young people in the area, not just old relics like us."

But I refused. I couldn't live an independent life in a wooded, rural place without bus transportation.

Bus transportation. I shot up from the pillow. That was what I needed to find out about today—routes to and from the guild.

"Breakfast, Sally," I commanded. I went back to the kitchen and opened the refrigerator. Yesterday Mom had packed the shelves with Muenster cheese, grapefruit, Tab, carrots, eggs, all my necessities. After the supply ran out, I would call and have a week's worth of groceries delivered. Still, I would have to locate the grocery store to pick up last-minute items. I knew the address of the store, but would need to learn the route.

Within an hour I'd eaten, phoned the transit company, dressed, and thumped my way downstairs and outside my building. At the corner of Bigelow Boulevard and Centre Avenue, my cane clanked against the metal pole that must hold the bus sign. What service—just a hundred feet from my door. Yet there would be other challenges—transferring to a second bus and then finding the way to work from my drop-off spot in Bridgeville. I'd have to pray that the bus driver or a kind pedestrian would point me in the right direction.

Well, I'd found the starting line. I'd worry about the rest of the bus trip tomorrow. The limited service today, Sunday, let me off the hook. Nevertheless, as I tapped my way back to the apartment, dread crept inside me.

I flopped onto my bed, pulled out my Braille textbook, and began to plan a lesson. The day shimmered with heat, slowing me, loosening my thoughts. Memories spilled out—other lesson plans, writing assignments spread like patchwork on the green vinyl couch in my beach apartment. My fiancé, Tom, beside me, reading Lawrence Durrell.

"Read these," I'd said, handing him essays from Chris and Julie, two of my third-grade students. "Their metaphors compete with his"—I nodded toward his book—"don't you think?"

He'd read, then smiled, not answering.

I sighed. He'd been a quiet one, that man—still water, but unfortunately not deep. Why was I thinking about him? Our engagement was over, and all to the good. I was remembering him because I had no one now: not my lifelong best friend, old "Lone Egg" Brian, still in California; not my college best friends, Carol, in New Jersey, and Sue, relocated out West; not my sweet, blind, best pal from the guild, Ken— gone, dead!

Dead! I still couldn't believe it, although I'd known for seven days.

"The diabetes." His mother's voice had choked through the telephone receiver. "Kidney failure."

Ken, dead. My mind couldn't, wouldn't absorb it. I could hear his voice, brimming with mischief, warmth.

The phone rang, and I jerked my hand, sending the Braille book sprawling. Damn! I was a mess even in the daylight!

I groped and found the telephone on the third ring. "Hobart?"

The dulcet tones of my cane instructor from the guild. "Sergeant Zimmerman!" I said, laughing.

"Shut up! Why haven't you called?" And before I could answer, she barked, "What are you doing for lunch?"

"I, ah, nothing."

"Good. I'll be right over. Big Mac okay?"

"Perfect," I said, hanging up. Good old Miss Zimmerman. Outside, granite; inside, eiderdown.

She arrived with her usual efficiency, then led me across the street to Schenley High School, empty on a Sunday afternoon. We would eat there, picnic style.

"You locate the bus stop?" she asked with the tone of an interrogator.

Fortunately, I could answer, "Yes." This woman made me want to be ever-alert, prepared, ready to do battle at a moment's notice.

"What about the opposite bus stop?"

She'd got me there. "Ah, no."

"And where's the grocery store?"

"Just below Centre and Craig Streets."

"Drugstore?"

I cleared my throat. Another glaring informational hole.

She sprang to her feet. "Grab on," she ordered, sticking her elbow into my stomach. She marched me to the corner, diagonally across from the bus stop I'd found, and showed me the best way to cross that intersection. Through the waning afternoon, she guided me around my new neighborhood, giving it focus, shape, sense. She showed me the alley and a grate near the drugstore, and a carpet on the sidewalk just before the grocery store. Tactile clues—how I loved them!

Gradually, I formed a mental map of the important places, the intersecting streets.

I repaid her with tuna salad and a beer. As shadows filled the apartment and I recalled the torment of the night before, I clung to the talk, the companionship. I tried to turn on lights discreetly, not wanting to shift Miss Zimmerman into a departure mode.

"Gotta go," she said, despite my efforts. She dropped her plate and glass into the sink. "I'll pick you up tomorrow."

"Are you sure?" I asked, relishing the offer. "I probably should get oriented to the buses." My words lacked conviction. An inner voice whispered, "Just not yet. Maybe in a day or two."

"Nonsense. You can practice the buses on your afternoon off." She opened the door. "Be ready at seven-thirty."

"Thanks," I said, saluting.

"Knock that off!" she snapped.

I laughed and waved. I closed the door and rested my cheek against it. Good old Miss Zimmerman.

"Okay," I turned and announced to the hollow room. "A bath to stimulate the sleep impulses. Then Braille practice to bore myself into slumber."

I turned on the bath water. Talking out loud to myself reined in my nerves. But soon it would make me a complete eccentric, and I'd lose any chance of fitting into sighted society.

❧ 3 ❧

As I caught a blurry glimpse of the floor at the Greater Pittsburgh Guild for the Blind, I remembered my first dreadful day here five months before. The rainy weather had matched my internal misery, and I'd dragged myself inside as if heading to the gallows. Now I entered happily, with the warm sun on my back. Trainee to teacher. The reversal made me giddy, giddy at the elasticity of human beings. The weak became strong. I hoped I could handle the new role. At least this place was familiar, unlike my apartment building.

"Sally!" someone called, and clasped my hand. "How was your vacation?"

I recognized the voice of my former counselor, Emily Feldstein, and saw her white pants. "Relaxing," I said. "Nice."

Next I saw a hazy yellow skirt. "Welcome, Sally." It was Ruth Becher, former teacher of Braille and techniques of daily living, now Education Department chairperson. "We're meeting in the conference room."

Mrs. Becher's greeting was surprisingly cool, but I

decided she was only being professional. I tapped up the stairs beside Miss Zimmerman, whom I was trying my best to call Gail. I took a seat between Emily and her and pulled out my knitting. From the bumps and jingling keys and jewelry, I could tell that the table was filling. I cocked my head, hoping to see enough of somebody to recognize him or her. Usually, if I was standing, I had a blurry view of the lower halves of people and objects. Sitting, I could tilt back my head and accomplish the same thing—identifying people by the color of their skirts or pants, the shapes of their legs. But today everyone was out of my three-foot sight range.

The talk in the room swelled, and the temperature rose. I knitted and purled, while my stomach did loops of its own.

Gail leaned on the arm of my chair and spoke in her throaty alto. "Some mobility instructors got very tan on vacation, Sally."

A man laughed. "I was at the Jersey shore."

I turned and whispered to Gail. "Who is that?"

"You remember Chuck Tedeshi, don't you?"

I didn't answer. In turning, I'd glimpsed her red top. My mind had tumbled back to another red shirt, another person who had leaned on my chair in this very room. Ken, always ready to mutter a wisecrack, to comment on my perfume, to propose a walk to the

15

local bar for beer. I wouldn't care that he wasn't here beside me if only he were out there in the suburbs of Pittsburgh, plodding along the sidewalks, like me.

"You okay, Sally?" asked Emily.

I was about to speak when all conversation stopped, and the room hushed. I could only assume that the director, Dr. Foyer, was entering and taking his place at the head of the table.

"How are you?" he asked.

A few people answered. "Fine." "Not bad." "Good, thanks."

"Welcome back," continued Dr. Foyer. "We have newcomers. Sally, why don't you begin the introductions around the table."

Four other new staff people identified themselves, and I put together the names of the missing. I hadn't known any of them well.

I touched Emily's arm. "Is there always this big a turnover?"

"Sometimes," she said. "Demanding job, mediocre pay."

After an hour we received our assignments. Mine was to orient an eighteen-year-old girl, Claire Robb, a student, blinded in an auto accident. After lunch I was to work with a group of trainees to evaluate their Braille skills. I picked up my cane and aimed for downstairs.

The women's dorm felt as comfortable as loose jeans. I paused by my old room and ran my fingers over the door. Something of me was still here, still a trainee, and I didn't want to forget that.

I found Claire in the bedroom next to mine, the one I'd shared with another trainee, Jenny. I wondered if Claire would be anything like my old roomie, at first shy and self-conscious, then alive and confident, awakened by the training.

"Claire?" I called, knocking on her door.

I heard someone stand. "Here," she answered.

"I'm Miss Hobart," I said, and fumbled for her hand. "I'm going to orient you this morning. Want to take my arm?"

I placed her hand on my left arm and stepped out of the room. Claire was slender, not as tall as I, but still above average height.

"You a little nervous?" I asked.

"No," she said. "I'm fine."

"I was overwhelmed my first day here," I admitted.

Stunned would be more accurate. But Claire was not the walking zombie I'd been. She seemed more composed, serious, not like me *or* Jenny.

Out in the hall, Claire paused. "You're using a cane."

"Yes, I'm blind, except for a small bit of sight. Trust me, I won't bump you into anything." I squeezed her hand, hoping to reassure her, then took a deep breath to reassure myself.

Gail would get a kick out of my orienting someone to this building. I'd tried her sorely when she performed this same task.

"Now touch the wall on your left. That's the north. If you trail that wall past the next room and make a right turn, you'll find the hall to the women's bathroom."

For the next two hours I led Claire around, allowing her to explore all she wanted.

"The more I put my bare hands, stockinged feet in contact with the environment, the better I memorize it," I said.

So Claire and I inched along, touching, laying endless fingerprints on walls, doors, desks, and chairs. When we reached the dining room, we took a break for tea.

"Do you mind telling me how old you are?" Claire asked.

I laughed. "On the wrong side of twenty-five," I said. "Almost twenty-six. Age is hard to judge by voice."

She clinked her cup on the saucer. "Have you been blind all your life?"

This trainee was interviewing me, as if she were the teacher. I wondered if she'd have more confidence in a sighted staff member, then brushed aside the thought. "No. I've been blind for about a year and a half," I answered.

"Really? You do so well," she said.

I patted her arm and stood. "And so will you. That's what this program is all about."

I led her back to her room, and turned to leave. But Claire had another question. "How did you become blind?"

"The blood vessels in my retinas kept breaking. That happens to diabetics, but I don't have diabetes," I explained. "Every three weeks, my left or right eye would bleed. Every hemorrhage reduced my sight— it's taken about two years." I checked my Braille watch. "Well, gotta go. Talk to you later."

I made my way to the Braille room, thinking about Claire. Maybe I would be a good role model for her.

What a shock it must have been to see one minute and be blind the next. For all the anguish I experienced these two years, losing my sight week by week, month by month, I preferred my way of going blind to Claire's. I'd had time to adjust gradually.

I sipped another cup of tea and chomped my carrot-stick lunch, as usual starving my stomach into submission, trying to maintain my ideal weight. I pulled out my assessment sheets. The Claire assignment had gone well. I hoped the next would go as smoothly.

A half hour later, Mrs. Becher delivered two young men to my door. I shook their hands and directed them to Ken's and my old seats. I gave them papers with different Braille letters and asked them to identify the number of dots.

"This is tough," said Eddie Solomon from my seat.

"These bumps are microscopic," complained Scott Horner, the man in Ken's chair.

I smiled. He sounded a bit like old Ken. "Don't you know that as many wonders can be experienced through the microscope as through the telescope?" Both men laughed.

Scott stretched back in the chair. "You don't say!"

"Yes," I continued. "Braille is one of the little wonders of the modern world. But few have the privilege of enjoying it. You two, however, have this rare opportunity for fifteen whole weeks."

"Wow! Lucky us," said Scott.

I laughed. Good sense of humor. A positive attitude. Scott was off to a great start.

For the rest of the day I measured sensitivity to the microscopic dots and evaluated Braille-reading levels. I sat on this desk top, working with these adults, as easily as I'd stood, teaching my third graders in California. The afternoon flew by.

As the last students left, Chuck Tedeshi knocked on the door. "Some of us are going out for dinner. Want to come?"

"Gee, I'd love it. Let me ask Gail."

"She's coming," he said, jingling his car keys. "Meet you out front."

I tossed my knitting and Braille text into a bag, then hurried to the ladies' room. I washed my face and hands and put on new lipstick and blush, keeping track of the number of strokes per cheek. Oh, how good this day had been! I was teaching again and socializing with other teachers. With a gap of only one school year, I was back in the classroom, somewhere I had never expected to be again. And it felt terrific.

~ 4 ~

The week passed quickly. I grew better acquainted with trainees and staff and helped to group my students into the proper Braille classes. None of the trainees who'd been born blind—the congenitally blind—needed additional Braille help. They'd been reading the "microscopic" dots for years, and their fingers flew across the page, speeding ahead of me by an enviable one hundred words a minute or so. I began to hold their accomplishments in awe.

Mrs. Becher, whom I was supposed to call Ruth, asked if I'd teach a section each of two other classes: visualization and abacus. During my training, I'd become a champ at adding, subtracting, multiplying, and dividing on the abacus, a small device that used rows of movable beads for calculation. Visualization was a class solely for the people who'd seen at some time in their lives, the adventitiously blind. The course covered ways of using the visual memory to aid in daily tasks.

Mrs. Becher's request pleased me. Not only did I relish the variety in subject matter but I appreciated the show of confidence. All week I had been sensing a coldness in Mrs. Becher. Now I chalked the iciness up to my imagination.

I packed the teacher's manuals in my satchel and prepared to leave. I pushed up the crystal of my Braille watch: 5 p.m.

Here I stood on the brink of a weekend, and not a single person to share it with. I could hole up in my apartment and prepare lessons. But with the working part of my life going so well, I wanted to ignite the social part.

I leaned against the wall. I knew one datable man,

Ted, a friend from Bucknell who'd helped me find the apartment. Since then he'd passed the bar exam and, unfortunately, moved to Washington, D.C. But wait. There was his friend, Arnie, who'd leased me the apartment. In my brief contact with him, he'd seemed interesting and attractive. I could phone him to say how much I liked the place. A twist of the truth, but not the first lie uttered in the cause of romance!

Someone knocked on the door. "All of us mobility instructors want to go out tonight and talk shop," said Gail. "Could you catch a ride with Emily or take the bus?"

Thunder should have clapped. I was planning to test the bus next week—not today—not this soon.

"Sal?"

I shook off the grip of dread. "Sure. No problem," I lied. "Have fun."

I dropped into my desk chair and tried to collect myself. The bus. I'd rather cocoon in this office all weekend.

Maybe I could catch Emily. I reached for my cane, but reconsidered. Emily might ask why I didn't take the bus.

Terror. That was why. I had taken buses in the training program, but never without Gail Zimmerman monitoring the trip. Well, I had to face it. I had planned to get mentally prepared first, but there wasn't time.

I took a deep breath and phoned the transit authority for the schedule. A 41C in about fifteen minutes. To get to the stop, I had to hurry down Station Avenue, across two streets, along one long block, and over the tracks to Railroad Street. A minute later, I tore out of the building and turned east. I whipped my cane left and right and charged ahead, determined, a woman with a mission. The motion gave order to my trembling, and I snapped across each street, adrenaline pumping, attention razor-sharp. Over the tracks and up onto the sidewalk—thunk. My cane banged the bus pole.

I checked my watch—5:19, exactly one minute after the bus was due. Damn. Could I have missed it? I hadn't heard the grinding sound of a bus as I approached. I shifted my weight. The next one wouldn't arrive until 6:02. Whatever would I do till then?

Then I smelled the exhaust of a bus, heard the motor, the thump of the doors opening.

"41C?" I called.

"Yes, miss," said the driver.

I aimed for his voice, found the first step with the tip of my cane, and lifted my foot.

"Not so fast, young lady," a man exiting snapped.

"Sorry," I said, jumping back, face flushing. Wake up, Sally! People *exit*, not just enter a bus.

"All clear, miss," announced the driver.

I clomped up the steps. "Transfer, please," I said, dropping in my money. "Will you tell me when we arrive at Fifth and Smithfield?" I asked.

"Sure thing."

People piled in behind me, pressed against me. I was taking too long. "Could you tell me where there's an empty seat?"

"Right behind me," he said.

I dropped onto the hard vinyl cushion and sighed. Success, at least on the first leg of the trip.

Or was it? The bus strained and lurched forward, and I worried that I was going in the wrong direction. I leaned toward the driver. "Excuse me."

He didn't hear. He was speaking to someone else. And my voice had as much volume as a four-year-old's.

But wait. I'd asked him to announce my stop. So I must be going the right way, or he would have sent me to another bus. I sat back. Now calm down, I told myself.

Within minutes, a new worry emerged. What if he forgot all about me in the congested downtown traffic? Gail advised keeping up a running conversation with the driver, but he was already in a steady tête-à-tête with another passenger.

I closed my eyes to rest and to forestall other conversation. I would listen for my chance to engage the driver. At the same time, I would meditate, pray, pursue tranquillity.

On the parkway the bus swayed and rocked. Slowly the tension eased out of me. I rubbed the back of my neck. Things were seldom as bad as I feared. Dread —the fiercest enemy.

When I heard the bus enter the tunnel, I thought of a strategy for engaging the driver. I leaned forward and asked, "Will any 61 bus take me to the Oakland neighborhood?"

"Yes," he said. "And any 71 also."

As the bus slowed in the rush-hour jam, I wondered again if the driver would remember me. I couldn't think of anything to say, so I coughed and cleared my throat—little reminders that I needed his help.

"Your stop, miss," he said finally.

Five minutes past six o'clock. "Oh, thanks!" I cried, standing. I tapped to the steps, my nerves propelling words from my mouth. "I don't know how you can remember. Gosh. That's really not a bad trip. Thanks."

I descended the steps and inched ahead through the clutter of pedestrians. The cane tip dropped. Fifth Avenue.

Five minutes later, I caught a second bus—not the express, which would take me a hundred feet from my home, but the local. Twenty minutes after that, I stepped out at Bigelow and Forbes, and in fifteen minutes more I was home sweet home. It was 6:40. The trip had taken twice the time it took by car, but that was okay—I'd made it!

I pitched my cane under the bed and clasped my hands in the air. "Good girl." Triumph! Look out, world!

I walked to the kitchen to make dinner. I plopped butter in a pan and listened until it sizzled. I cracked two eggs and tossed them in, stirring. When the liquid began to grow solid, I lowered the heat and kept stirring. I found a Tab and ate the eggs straight from the pan. I scoured the pan till it was egg-free, smooth as new to the touch.

Then I slipped into a chair and smiled. If I could conquer the bus, I could take on the next challenge —Arnie.

⪬ 5 ⪭

I held the phone on my lap, fingers poised to dial the number. But I couldn't summon the courage. Flirting, placing myself in a man's way, was not so easy now. A sighted man and woman could exchange meaningful looks without risking anything. If I called Arnie,

I put myself more on the line than if I just riveted him with lingering eye contact.

"Come on, you coward!" I whispered. I'd gone to the trouble of finding his telephone number through directory assistance. What could I lose? Self-esteem, self-confidence, self-respect.

I massaged my temples. Thinking used to be a less common operation of my mind, and I liked it better that way.

"Nothing comes from nothing," Daddy always said.

I swallowed, fired off a volley of prayers, then dialed.

"Hello, Arnie? This is Sally Hobart. I rented the apartment—"

"Hey, how are you?"

He remembered me. Oh, thank heaven. Maybe I wouldn't make a total fool of myself.

"Great. I love the place," I lied.

"I was just about to walk to Craig Street for ice cream," he said. "You free to come?"

He was going for ice cream. Was I free? "Um, sure."

"I'll be there in fifteen minutes," he said.

Fifteen minutes, but my hair—a shower. "Terrific," I said. "Should I meet you downstairs?"

"Don't bother. I'd like to see what you've done to the old place."

What I'd done? "Fine," I said, dropping the phone. I banged it back on the table. How could I resurrect myself and remove the dust balls in fifteen minutes?

I rushed, which was never advisable now that I was blind. Wham! My hip conked the corner of the chest. Pain shot down my leg like a torpedo through water. I washed my face, brushed my teeth, all the while holding a cold washcloth on the throbbing welt. Then I whipped the dust mop around the rugs and tossed all debris into the closet. Makeup—I'd almost forgotten.

"For someone who doesn't see herself, you sure care a lot about how you look." The teasing words of my ophthalmologist, Dr. Taggart, came back to me.

Vanity, vanity. But being well groomed, properly put together was almost more important to me, blind. I didn't want people to think I was disheveled, mismatched, because I couldn't see, didn't know better.

Too soon I heard Arnie's knock. I opened my cologne and pressed the rim to my neck, sloshing it on. I'd either anesthetize him immediately or bring on his asthma.

I struck a casual pose and opened the door. "Hi," I said.

"Hi."

A good beginning.

He strode past me into the large room. "Great rugs!" he exclaimed. "Were you in Arizona?"

"Yes, but not to buy the rugs. They're from my grandfather's house—pretty old, I think."

He appreciated other things about the room and commented. I liked him, his composed, interested, straightforward manner.

"Ready to go?" he asked.

I picked up my keys and cane and went out ahead of him. I felt comfortable on the carpeted stairs and hurried down the two flights. Dusk had fallen, but I was still warm enough in my short skirt and T-shirt.

"Indian summer," I said. "Don't you love it?"

Not brilliant, but my remark kept the conversation idling till it shifted into gear.

"Yeah," he said.

We walked down the hill beside each other, me tapping away, concentrating on the hazy three feet of sidewalk I could make out. I listened for parallel cars—easy enough on Centre Avenue with constant traffic. And I groped for something else to say.

Arnie stopped. "Can I help?" he asked. "I mean, you're doing fine, but let me know."

I smiled. "May I take your arm? It would make talking easier."

It would also make checking him out easier, but I

didn't say that. Arnie was tall enough for me—always an issue—slim, with a nice muscle in his arm.

"Anything I should know about leading you?" he asked.

"Just pause or tell me when there are ups or downs," I said. "Sorry. I should have explained."

Gail had always told me to take the initiative. "Use people like taxicabs," she'd said. "Tell them you can get from place A to place B on your own, but when you come to place C, you may need their arm, their guidance."

At the corner, Arnie turned to face me. "How'd you become blind, Sally?"

My name in his baritone sounded nice.

I told him the details, and our conversation began to flow swift and steady. Arnie asked how much I could see and what work I was doing. He seemed really interested in the details, which I found unusual for a man, or unusual for the men I knew, Tom and the California crew. And Arnie wasn't afraid to speak of blindness by its proper name. So many people danced around the word, saying "sightless" or "visionless" instead.

At the ice cream store, I ordered English toffee, a double dip.

On the way home, it was my turn to ask the questions. Arnie explained that he was a third-year law student at the University of Pittsburgh. He had a sister and a widowed mom who lived nearby, and aspirations of becoming "a big shot." He laughed when he said this.

When we stepped under the awning at the Schenley Arms, my building, I asked if he wanted to come up.

"No thanks," he said. "I'm driving with some friends to D.C. for a protest tomorrow. I'll give you a call." He squeezed my arm and went off.

A protest? Against the Vietnam War, I supposed.

I pulled open the heavy door of the building. Because my brother, Bobby, and his two best pals from Conyngham were in Saigon, I'd been ignoring the mounting opposition to the war. Besides, I'd had no time to be political. For nearly two years, I'd been waging my own battle, trying to retain some sight. I'd hardly tuned in to the television coverage, and I wasn't certain how I stood on the war. Should we be fighting in Vietnam or not?

But I was sure of one thing. I'd interacted with a man again, flirted, and the experience was not all that different blind from the way it had been sighted.

I tilted my head back and ran up the stairs. Risky, but exhilarating. Fortunately, I had enough sight to halt before ramming an elderly tenant.

I unlocked the door and searched for my teacher's manuals.

"Arnie!" I said, feeling a grin crack from earlobe to earlobe. I didn't know if I was ready to date anyone seriously again, but I'd enjoyed being with Arnie, and I hoped he *would* call.

6

On Monday morning I began the actual teaching. I cocked back my head to see something of my first group entering for Braille class, all five totally and newly blind. Claire was among them, as well as nineteen-year-old Eddie, a student who'd been injured in a hunting accident, and Scott, who'd been an automobile salesman before blinding himself in a suicide attempt. I shivered, just as I had when the secretary had read me his record.

The two others, both men, were an English professor blinded by diabetes and a local boxer who had detached both retinas in a fight. They filed in like prisoners of war, four of the five blinded overnight. My throat tightened. How could they go on?

I pushed aside the memory of their histories and directed them to seats. "Instead of giving you Braille textbooks today, I want to begin with writing. The machine in front of you is called a Perkins Brailler."

Mrs. Becher always began teaching Braille with reading, not writing. I hoped she would approve of this departure from her approach.

I placed each student's index, middle, and ring fingers on six of the keys. The boxer, Lou, had rough, hairy hands that trembled. I felt a pang. How must he feel to have chosen a career that destroyed his sight?

Stop it, I told myself, taking a deep breath. I addressed the class. "The Braille alphabet is based on different arrangements of six dots," I explained. "With the six keys that you are touching now, you can write the entire alphabet, anything."

"Another *Canterbury Tales*," suggested the English professor, Dr. Allen. He had a slight whistle when he spoke.

"Huh?" asked Lou.

Dr. Allen rubbed his hands together. "A great literary work about love, marriage, good, evil."

Eddie, the teenager, groaned and drew out the word, "Okay."

I directed them to the three remaining keys, which moved the embosser forward or backward or moved the paper up.

They experimented with all nine keys, filling the room with a dull, drumming sound.

"The letter 'A' is dot one. Press it with your left index finger, then push the forward space key with your thumb. Now feel what you've written."

In this way I introduced the first five letters of the alphabet. I made them feel each one, over and over again.

"Now write as many words as you can, using those letters. When you finish, take out the paper and try to decipher your work." I hoped they'd recognize their own words faster than words from a text.

Dutifully all five batted out words, sounding like a pack of dogs thumping tails. Lou, Eddie, and Scott joked, tipped back in their chairs, gave the impression of being twice as many people. They were not as broken down as I'd expected.

"Hey, Eddie, how do you spell 'ad'?" asked Lou.

"Don't know. Ask the professor."

Eddie's barbs were not subtle. What was going on between him and Dr. Allen? I swallowed. Hostility between two grown men required different refereeing from conflict between two third-grade boys. I'd managed thirty-eight kids without mutiny; surely I could manage five adults.

Claire and Dr. Allen worked steadily, letting few words escape their lips.

"Hey, Miss H."

I turned to Scott.

"You don't mind if I call you that? Rumor has it you're my age." He laughed. "How can I treat you like an old-maid, girdle-wearing schoolteacher?"

I smiled. "Well, you've got the old-maid part right."

Rumor had it? Ken had always teased me by claiming to employ spies to gather information. Scott was like him—same aptitude for teasing, same energy, same humor. What could have happened to drive him to shoot himself?

I moved to the middle of the room to get a hazy look at him and the others. Scott appeared to be large, out-of-shape. Eddie looked tall and lean, while Lou was shorter, more square and solid. Dr. Allen had an average build and seemed to be wearing a jacket and tie. Claire looked as I'd imagined her that first day, tall and slender.

I heard the trio on my right, Eddie, Scott, and Lou, removing papers from their Braillers.

"You expect me to read this?" cried Eddie.

"Letter by letter, word by word," I said. I reached over and touched his shoulder. "You ran track. Take it lap by lap."

"Track was fun," he snapped.

I'd been insensitive, bringing up track. This boy had been an athlete. He would have such an adjustment. Unless he was willing to hold someone's arm, he would never run again. I began to understand why he shot poisoned arrows.

"If you were a pal, Miss H.," began Scott, "you would let us space between each letter in the words."

"Complaints, complaints," I said, teasing.

But didn't he have a right to complain? Didn't they all—every one of them under thirty-five?

I was luckier. I still had a little sight. I had a job and confidence from the training. But give them the fifteen-week program, and they would be okay, too.

The bell rang, and I waited for my next Braille group. My other three Braille classes went smoothly. All the trainees seemed pleasant.

After lunch I held my first visualization class. Claire, Dr. Allen, Lou, Eddie, and Scott were among the trainees. Leon Garrett, a seventeen-year-old who had lost his vision in a gun fight, was new to me.

"Visualization is central to everything you're learning," I began, "spoken communication, sensory training, mobility, techniques of daily living. Your memory can help you to picture the food on your plate, an intersection, an image on the movie or television screen."

I turned to Claire and tapped her hand. "What do you do when you meet a person?"

"Face him. Say how nice it is to meet him."

"Good," I said. "Anything else?"

"Extend my hand," offered Dr. Allen.

"Right," I said.

"I imagine what they look like," announced Scott, "then try to get a description."

I clapped my hands. "Good. You form an automatic picture based on someone from your past whom the speaker sounds like. If you can get a description, all the better. First mental pictures are hard to erase, so you want the description as soon as possible."

"If anyone wants a few clues about what Miss H. looks like," said Scott, "talk to me after class. I already got the scoop."

I smiled. "Just picture a tall Jackie Kennedy." I laughed then. "But this brings up an important point: Famous people can be good references in helping to visualize."

"I'm the spitting image of Paul Newman," announced Lou.

"A bald Paul," said Eddie, laughing.

"What about the rest of you? Whom do you resemble?"

One by one they pinpointed a well-known person.

"If you want to know what someone looks like, you could feel her face," suggested Lou.

Eddie hit the table. "I hate that! How the heck does that tell anyone anything?"

"It lets you know if the person has a beard, mustache, glasses," said Dr. Allen, "sharp nose, long hair—"

"Okay, so I'm wrong," interrupted Eddie. "But I know a lot of people who'd hate me mauling their faces with my grubby hands."

Eddie was trying to control his temper. I admired his frankness. Sometimes blind people are reluctant to disagree, to show anger. We try to make up for being blind by being overly agreeable.

I leaned against the wall. "How do the rest of you feel about touching the face?"

"It's a stereotype," said Scott.

Claire dinged her bracelet on the Brailler. "It gives some information, but it shows mostly what a person feels like, not what he looks like."

"Tell the guy who wants you to touch his face that you don't need to," offered Scott. "You can tell what he looks like by the way he smells."

Everybody laughed, even Claire and Dr. Allen.

I decided to redirect the discussion. "By talking to a person, you can judge height. By taking his arm, you can judge something about shape, physique, and form a picture." My thoughts strayed to Arnie, the feel of his arm, the walk for ice cream.

Scott leaned back in his seat. "I hate to break it to you, Miss H.," he said. "The arm isn't a body part that determines shape."

"But we'd get slugged if we touched those parts," exclaimed Lou.

Again, everyone howled.

Dr. Allen rubbed his hands together again. "Touching is generally taboo in our culture. It suggests intimacy."

"What's wrong with that?"

There was a pause while everyone identified the speaker: quiet Leon. Then the room erupted.

"Yeah, you got a problem with that?" asked Eddie.

"No," said Dr. Allen. "It's the life goal of every one of us, the daily quest."

"Take it easy, Professor. You're married. The rest of us aren't," snapped Eddie. "Besides, Miss H. is our teacher, not you."

"It's okay, Eddie," I said, touching his wrist. "Dr. Allen is just contributing to the class." I still didn't know why Eddie had it in for that man. I squeezed Eddie's hand. "Class dispatched."

As they shuffled out, I mused. Intimacy, "the life goal . . . the daily quest." Well, my intimate one-hour walk with Arnie had drifted into my thoughts more than once during the past three days. I sighed. Would I have an evening of tedious class preparations, or would Arnie phone tonight?

7

Arnie did phone. He dropped by with a quart of English toffee ice cream, which was becoming a vice. And every fourth or fifth night during the next few weeks he came over, always after studying or demonstrating, always accompanied by ice cream or something calorically sinful.

Were these dates? I couldn't be sure. But the pace, the informality, the lack of pressure suited me.

In early October he asked me on an official date.

"You interested in going to a movie Friday night?" he said. "Figure you should get in for half price." He laughed.

I smiled, but shook my head. "My friend Carol is coming in from New Jersey. Sorry." Ted, an acquaintance of Arnie's from law school, was also coming in, but Arnie didn't seem to know. Ted had invited me to a party and had found a date for Carol.

The party was a fiasco. No sooner had we arrived than Ted said, "Hey, I'll be right back." He squeezed my hand.

I smiled and nodded. Then reality struck. I stood

where he'd left me, not knowing where he'd gone, not knowing how to maneuver in the unfamiliar, dimly lit house, not knowing a soul besides Carol and her date, who'd disappeared into another room.

When I could see, my dates and I hadn't stayed together like Siamese twins. Tom always had gone off with his friends to shoot pool or throw darts.

But I was blind now, and this was my first huge party outside of the guild. The music, noise, the mob of people overwhelmed me. Within minutes my emotions churned—rage against Ted for leaving me, loathing for myself. I stood, dark as a storm cloud, trapped against a wall.

But then someone spoke. "How are you?"

"Fine," I answered, feeling my limp body straighten, my cheeks spread into a smile.

The man who had spoken touched my arm. "I wasn't talking to you. Sorry. I was just saying something to Jane here."

Oh, I was pathetic, so inept. I flipped my fingers through my hair, then checked my watch. Impossible! We'd been here longer than fifteen minutes.

I shifted my weight to the other foot. I hated this: standing here, poised for someone to address me, awkward as an eighth grader hoping to be asked to dance. I'd never before known dependency in social situations. At a huge party, I'd been the person who'd passed hors d'oeuvres, introduced people, acted as assistant hostess. I'd possessed all the skills necessary to manage a gathering like this—but not now, not blind.

Ted came back then, and I tried to shake the funk, but the damage had been done. My emotions were tangled in knots, and I couldn't muster the appropriate chitchat. Ted went to get me a drink and stayed away even longer.

I stood alone again, worrying about everything. If Ted ever returned with the drink, I'd have to use the bathroom. How would I find that? And I was famished. Why hadn't I asked him to bring food?

An arm slid around me. "You look as miserable as I feel," Carol said.

"You're not having fun?"

She groaned. "This is about as much fun as an appendectomy without anesthesia."

I laughed for the first time that night.

Carol stayed with me through the rest of the interminable party. She missed Mike, a man from her hometown whom she had been growing serious about. Ted returned periodically, and I displayed as much personality as a brick.

Ted and Carol's date dropped us at the Schenley Arms. Probably they were as relieved to separate as we were. Behind the apartment door, Carol and I fumed. "Save me from a trial lawyer," she grumbled.

" 'Why is a twenty-six-year-old woman like you still living at home with her parents?' Ugh! Those were two of the most insensitive guys I've ever met."

"Maybe," I said. But the tragedy of the evening was that I hated myself, the new me, not Ted.

"We should have grabbed our coats and a taxi," Carol exclaimed.

I nodded and went to the kitchen to pour us each a glass of wine. "Oh, well," I said, "Ted is balding anyhow."

Carol laughed, then touched my knee. "So you cared about him a little?"

I shook my head. "Not really. He's a datable man I've seen. It might have been nice if we'd connected." I clenched my hand into a tight ball. "Tonight I sure wanted to connect—my fist, his nose!"

We laughed.

If I'd been more experienced, blind, I would have handled the party better. I would have anticipated the difficulties, and that alone would have taken away some of the sting. I would have tried to get oriented, or I would have insinuated myself into the one measly conversation at hand. At the very least I would have asked Ted to check back with me often, in case I needed something.

The evening did have one positive outcome, however. I learned that a huge crowded party would never be easy for me. No matter what the shape of my psyche, I would have trouble making my way through a sea of bodies. Either I would strike food or drink from a hand or I would bump an off-limits body part.

I had told Carol the truth. I had no romantic feelings for Ted. For that reason, it was easy to make an excuse the next time he phoned.

It wouldn't be so easy, however, to avoid big parties for the rest of my life, but I resolved to do it.

~≈ 8 ≈~

A few nights after the infamous party, Arnie brought me a pumpkin. Together we carved and laughed, retrieving the slimy pumpkin seeds. I gave him a bag of my favorite Halloween treats, candy corn, which I'd picked up earlier at the drugstore.

"Thanks," he said, leaning over the pumpkin and kissing me.

I'd been used to a quick kiss from him at the door, but now he kissed me again, a terrific kiss from a romantic movie. Then he moved his finger along my nose and lips, my cheeks. "You're so pretty." He paused. "Do you ever wonder what I look like?"

I nodded. "Sometimes, when I've been standing and you've been sitting, I've tried to peek, but it's too blurry. I know you have a nice build."

He played with my hair. "What do you think I look like?"

I hesitated. Appearance was such an important part of who a person was. "Well, I know there's no mustache or beard, a nice nose and mouth, no glasses." I smiled. "Um, I picture dark, curly hair . . ."

He smacked his legs. "Curly? Here. Feel." He grabbed my hand, and I felt thick, smooth, straight hair, like the coat of a German shepherd.

He stood, radiating anger like heat. "I gotta go."

I jumped up. "How'd I offend you, Arnie?"

"Curly hair," he snapped. "Because I'm Italian. Why didn't you add 'greasy' while you were at it?"

I reached for his arm.

"Forget it!" He pulled away. "I have to carve crosses for the protest march."

"Arnie, it's just that your voice reminds me of a guy I went to high school with. His hair was curly, and he wasn't Italian."

He stomped out the door and seemed to take the heat with him.

I rested my hand on the knob, then walked stiff and stilted to the middle of the room. I took a deep breath. Arnie was hard and uncompromising. I'd heard that quality in him before, but it was directed at the Administration in Washington, the military. And his comments, harsh though they were, had made sense, had seemed reasonable. Because of him, I now listened more to the news and had begun to oppose the Vietnam War.

Still, I had loyalties to my brother and his friends there. Bobby had a clerical job in Saigon, as safe a position as there was in that country. Occasionally he drove officers around in a jeep, and that was more dangerous. But his two best friends from Conyngham, guys I'd joked with all my life, were helicopter pilots and were shot at every day. I wasn't ready to join Arnie in marching. Besides, I was too busy just getting a normal life going again.

I rubbed my neck. Why was I trying to justify my nonpolitical self? That wasn't what had made Arnie mad. I picked up the pumpkin and placed it on the windowsill. Carving crosses? What did that mean? Carving the names of dead American soldiers?

My foot hit the forgotten bag of candy corn. I sat down, opened it, and nibbled. Did Arnie see the irony in his sculpting a pumpkin minutes before he turned the knife to crosses? He had a sense of humor, but I wasn't sure he could laugh at himself.

I put the candy on a shelf and picked up my papers to grade. I hadn't been making an ethnic slam. Arnie had misunderstood. I sighed. How many bruised feelings had there been between Tom and me? I marveled that anyone ever achieved the "life goal," intimacy.

Several days later, Arnie knocked on my door. I opened it and prepared for a rehashing of the curly-hair offense.

"Brought chocolate chip cookies," he announced, shaking a bag.

I brewed tea, poured it properly—no fingertip help—and we sat down and munched.

"Your birthday's coming up," he said. "What would you like to do?"

I licked the crumbs from my lips. "Go to the symphony," I said, speaking the first thing that came to mind.

"Good. I'll get tickets for Friday night." He thumped his cup down on the table. "Gotta go."

One kiss, sweet as liqueur, and he was gone.

So no rehash. Oh, well. I'd never talked out any fight with Tom. The squabbles just blew over until there were so many that they all blew back in our faces—with hurricane force.

The symphony. I smiled.

On October 17, my birthday, Arnie and I walked the six blocks to the Syria Mosque, home of the Pittsburgh Symphony. The orchestra played *Till Eulenspiegel* and one other piece I recognized, so I felt mighty cultivated. When we returned to the apartment, a friend down the hall surprised me with a birthday party. She'd invited a few residents of the Schenley Arms and two of my friends from work, Hannah Nelkin, a counselor, and Chuck Tedeshi, who lived around the corner. For two weeks now, Chuck had replaced Gail as my chauffeur back and forth to work.

Afterward Arnie gave me my presents. "An Elton John and a Paul Simon record," he explained. "Your collection needs some updating."

I laughed. He was right. "Thanks."

I opened something else that was round and hard and cool as glass. It sat on a small wooden stand. I turned to Arnie and cocked my head.

"A crystal ball to help with the future," he said. "Yours has been pretty uncertain."

I hugged him. I felt a catch in my throat, and my words faltered. Tom had never surprised me with special gifts, had never even remembered my birthday.

Arnie kissed me then, again a romantic movie kiss.

I kissed his nose. "Do you want something to drink?" I asked.

"No," he said, kissing me again. It was very nice. Yet I felt crowded and pushed, somehow upset. I pulled away.

Arnie stood and paced. The floorboards creaked.

Outside the window, the city rattled and screeched. Otherwise, the room was silent.

He turned to me. "When you can't see, how do you know if you're attracted to someone?" His voice was quiet but intent.

I sighed. An important question. One I had mostly feelings about, not answers.

"Several years before I lost my sight, I became less interested in a guy's appearance and more interested in his inside stuff," I began.

"So my good looks are lost on you."

I smiled, but there was no humor in his words.

"What does attract you?" His tone was that of a prosecutor.

"How a person acts, what he says, his sense of humor, ideas." I ran my fingers through my hair. "The physical attraction, well, I guess I could be committed to kissing before I really knew if I was physically attracted."

"Great," he said, pacing again. "You've just been kissing me."

"I like kissing you." The words came out in a whisper. Arnie seemed so angry. "I mean, I'm attracted to a nice physique, the way a person smells. It's embarrassing to talk about it. I like a man to feel strong . . ."

I was saying too much, but couldn't stop. "You

have a nice physique; you feel strong. But sometimes I could be kissing a guy already and then realize that the chemistry was missing. I might encourage him and then wish I hadn't."

"Is the chemistry there with me, Sally?"

I swallowed. "Yes."

"You don't act like it is," he said, and stormed out.

How could I explain to Arnie what I didn't understand myself? Part of me longed for male appreciation. But the failed romance with Tom made me reluctant to care so much again.

9

"Do you like that Arnie guy?"

I turned to Chuck as we sped along the parkway toward work Monday morning. "Yes," I said. "Why do you ask?"

"He's so serious-looking, serious-acting."

I slowed the movement of my knitting needles. "You don't know him. Besides, why would I care what he looked like?" I rubbed my nose from sheer annoyance. "As for the way he acts—my ex-fiancé was such a party guy that I prefer someone a little serious." I placed my knitting in the bag and shifted in the seat. "Truth is, I'm probably not going to see Arnie anymore."

And I didn't, not in the dating sense of the word, at any rate. Arnie did come and go in the Schenley Arms, but only because he'd transferred his attentions down the hall to the woman who'd thrown the birthday party. They were a much better match than Arnie and I had been. And I felt only the disappointment of one quickly forgotten.

October merged into somber, dreary November, fallen leaves heavy as soaked paper towels under my cane. Work enlivened me, and I found a friend like Ken in Chuck. We went to movies, ate pizza, and palled around together. He introduced me to a church three blocks from my apartment, the Community of Reconciliation. It was a multidenominational church, interracial and politically active.

As he guided me to a pew, I passed parishioner after parishioner singing at full volume. Exuberance like this I'd never witnessed in a church.

"You're overdressed," Chuck whispered. "Wear jeans next week."

A woman in front of us handed me a hymnal. "Verse three," she said.

"Sorry. Can't use it," I whispered, pointing to my eyes. "Blind."

"Oblivious," she said, taking my hand and tapping her chest. "Actually, I'm Rachel. Talk to you after the service."

That was the beginning of a new friendship. Rachel Berg. Widow for two weeks, mother of four—most of them about my age. Social worker. A woman with such zest for life that people flocked around her.

One wind-howling afternoon I worked with Leon and four other students.

"Homework, please," I said, taking the papers from their outstretched hands.

"I didn't have time to do it," said Leon.

I made a mental note to talk with him after class. This was the third assignment he'd failed to turn in.

I pulled open the Braille text and asked someone besides Leon to begin.

" 'Pre, um, scription, sub . . . sti . . . tution, um, loco . . . motion, se . . . cretion.' "

"Good job." These trainees were working on the shorthand form for "t-i-o-n." Like all my students, they'd learned the alphabet, numbers, and punctuation in Grade One Braille. The words and sentences in the text were growing longer and more complex.

"Leon? The next line, please."

"Ah . . ." he began.

While I waited, I wondered if he was having problems with neuropathy, numbing of the fingertips. "Can you read the first letter or any of it?" I asked.

" 'V,' " he said.

"Great. What about the other letters?"

" 'O-l-i-tion sign,' " he read easily.

I clapped my hands. "Way to go, Leon." No neuropathy, for sure. "So you've spelled the word . . . ?"

He didn't answer, so I said, " 'Volition,' right?"

"Yup."

"It'll get easier. Want to try the next word?"

Silence.

"What's the first letter, Leon?"

" 'E,' " he answered easily.

An idea was coming to me. "Can you read it letter by letter again?"

" 'E-x-h-a-u-s-tion sign.' "

"Good for you," I said. "And that spells . . . ?"

More silence. And I knew: Leon's problem wasn't the common one, separating the dots and recognizing the letters. His problem was more serious. Leon couldn't read. He must not have been able to read before he'd lost his sight.

I touched another trainee's hand. "Will you take the next word?"

I would postpone talking to Leon about homework until I'd spoken to Mrs. Becher. I had a plan.

As soon as class ended, I searched her out. I proposed that I work during lunch or any free pe-

54

riod with Leon, simply on reading. Because of my elementary-school background, she agreed, and Leon and I set to work that very day.

"You mind giving up your free time for this reading work, Leon?"

"Nope," he said.

"Would you tell me if you did, or would that seem impolite?"

"I'd tell you, Miss H." He gave a low chuckle. "Figure it's 'bout time I get some learning. Hard enough for a black man to find a job, let alone a blind black man. And if the buzzard can't read, well, that just cuts his wings altogether. So, Miss H., hit me with those letters."

I hit him with consonants first. He knew all those beginning sounds, so we turned to vowels—A-E-I-O-U.

The lunch hour passed, and I was hooked. I loved working with Leon, who was warm and funny and bright. I loved using skills from another job, another time. Day by day, teaching grew even more gratifying.

Claire, Dr. Allen, and Scott were my Braille stars. Eddie and Lou kept up, but the other three inhaled the work like fresh air. They advanced quickly into the shorthand form of Braille, called Grade Two, where one symbol could stand for a whole word, prefix, or suffix.

Scott wrote long homework essays, akin to journal

entries. I learned about his wife's infidelity with his best friend, about her sitting in this best friend's lap right in front of the newly blinded Scott. How could I correct the Braille and ignore the content?

One day I asked him to stay after class.

"What's up, teach?" he asked. "You sending a poor-work notice home to my mom and pop?"

I smiled and brushed his hand. "No. Your work is excellent. I'm just so sorry about the experiences you've described."

"They've been bummers, Miss H.," he said, and his voice sounded husky. "But everybody here's got a sad tale to tell, even you."

"I know." I hesitated, then continued. "One thing that helped me a lot was the counseling. Mrs. Feldstein is a gem." I waited, but he didn't say anything. "I guess I'm hoping that you discuss these issues with your counselor, too."

"You know, Miss H., you have a sexy voice."

I opened my mouth, but nothing came out. His words seemed to close the door on any more discussion.

"I'm sorry," Scott said. "My wife"—he cleared his throat—"my ex-wife, well, she's a drug. I can't live with her, I can't live without her." His voice cracked.

I reached out, but decided not to take his hand. My throat was so full, and tears threatened to spill down my cheeks.

Someone stepped into the doorway. "Miss Hobart, what's— Am I interrupting?"

I turned to face Ruth Becher. "No," I said. "I was just finishing up." I lowered my voice. "Scott, may I share your work with Mrs. Feldstein?"

He stood. "Sure. Why not?"

As soon as I heard his cane far enough down the hall, I heaved a loud sigh. "Oh, Mrs. Becher. That man's gone through so much."

"Undoubtedly," she said. Her tone was severe. "But you do him no good if you can't keep your professional distance."

The hair on my neck bristled. Words of defense stampeded my mind. I was the only blind person on staff, aside from a partially sighted male counselor. It was a struggle not to overempathize. But I'd been behaving properly. I'd suggested he talk to his counselor.

"You're right, of course," I said, swallowing my defense.

"In making the decision to hire you, we concluded that you could maintain your role as teacher," she continued, the words raw and cold.

I clenched my teeth. Ruth Becher didn't respect an admission of fault. She used it for further scolding. This quality provoked the rebel in me. I wanted to shout, "I *was* maintaining my role!"

The change in the woman, the coldness toward me,

was not my imagination. As a trainee, I'd been Princess Charming to her. As a member of her staff, one rung higher on the power ladder, I seemed to lose all charm.

In schools, as in most institutions, there was a hierarchy of power—director on top, department chairpersons next, teachers below, and students on the bottom. Yet I felt the friction now, not when I was a trainee. Had I been so grateful for any kindness then that I'd ignored the power issues? Or was I more threatening to Ruth Becher now that I had restored confidence, a restored career? Did she view me as an "uppity blind person" who should know her place?

I wasn't sure. I only knew that my feelings for her had changed; I couldn't respect her anymore. From now on, I'd have no trouble calling her by her first name.

Her voice cut through my angry thoughts. "Just teach him Braille, and don't let your feelings get in the way."

Her speech was an insult, but I sealed my lips.

"On another matter," she went on, "I see in the records that none of your Braille classes is keeping up the proper pace, except for this section with Scott. Why aren't you moving the other groups as quickly?"

My anger went from simmer to slow boil. "Those groups were getting bogged down. Any teacher would have stopped and reviewed. It wasn't wasted time,

Ruth. I showed them how to organize address books, recipes, labels." I was sounding too defensive, yet I had to explain. In the past I'd heard only praise for my teaching.

"You'll never finish all of Grade Two Braille this way."

I let out a breath. "Ruth, very few of my students will read novels in Braille. I want to give them as much as I can and not overwhelm them. This way they'll be able to use Braille to function independently."

I could feel her stiffen. "As your supervisor, I expect you to push all your students through the curriculum." She turned and walked out, leaving only her perfume and an enraged blind woman behind.

Chuck and a few other instructors always mimicked the way Ruth pronounced the long "u" vowel. "As your syupervisor . . ." I repeated the word, mocking her, then threw myself into a chair.

What was I going to do? I disagreed so totally with her approach. I had been in her most advanced Braille class, and two-thirds of the group couldn't keep up with the speed. Sweet old Ken, Jake, Pat, John—they all left the program planning never to touch another Braille dot. The result was that they were virtual illiterates—unable to keep telephone numbers, reminder lists, messages to themselves.

The rest of the day I fumed, thinking about my

options even as my students moved the abacus beads in math.

"Miss H.," called Scott, "you still here?"

"Yes," I said as if stepping from a deep fog. "Sorry."

"You want the professor to take over?" asked Eddie. "He's always tutoring Claire." He and Lou snickered.

"Shut up, you guys," snapped Claire.

Her words were bullets, and they amazed me. She'd been even-tempered, never hot or cold on any subject.

"Hey," I called, "let's calm down and avoid the bloodshed."

I kicked myself for daydreaming and allowing the hostilities to spark. I shoved aside the Braille dilemma and concentrated on abacus.

But when the class left, I prepared for battle. I was an experienced teacher. That I'd lost my sight did not mean I'd lost my judgment. Ruth Becher was well trained in the arena, but I'd meet her there head on and fight—down to the stumps of my fingertips.

❧ 10 ❧

"Dr. Foyer wants to see you in his office," announced the secretary from my doorway.

My stomach twisted tight as a spring. Gail, Hannah, and the sensory training teacher, Lyn Howard, clucked their tongues. Gail whistled "Taps."

"Funny," I said.

I took my cane and prepared to meet the commanding officer. On the second floor, I slid the tip of my cane along the left wall to find the third doorway. I inhaled, wet my lips, and knocked.

"Come in," he hollered, and I turned the knob. "Chair's on your right, Sally."

I glimpsed the forest green cushion and sat down. Dr. Foyer's chair creaked, and I pictured him sitting back, hands behind his head, elbows out. *He* had no worries.

"Sally," he began easily. "Understand you're feuding with Ruth Becher."

Just as I'd expected, Ruth had reported everything to him. Everything except my version of events.

"Ruth says you won't submit to her will or her way," he continued. "She's mightily perturbed."

It occurred to me that he was enjoying himself at my expense. Still, I repeated all that I'd said to Ruth and more.

"Two groups will definitely finish Grade Two," I said. "So will a few other people. My main concern is that they use the Braille when they leave."

I heard Dr. Foyer rise slowly. His footsteps moved around his desk and stopped in front of me. The blur of his blue suit loomed over me.

I awaited his reaction, feeling tics in my neck and cheek. He was silent. Important people didn't need to hurry.

"I completely agree with you," he said finally.

He agreed? I sat back, surprised. Relieved. He was on my side in this fight. I could continue to teach Braille my way.

"Will you speak to Ruth about this, then? Somehow I think she'll take it better from you."

"That's not necessary, honey."

My head shot up. Not necessary? What did he mean?

"Just teach the way you've been teaching," he went on. "Your instincts are perfect."

Perfect? Then why wouldn't he speak to Ruth for me? What was going on?

He lifted my chin with fatherly warmth. I caught sight of his navy pants, his thick, squat piano legs. "Say, Yes, ma'am, to Ruth, and teach your way." He handed me my cane, signaling the end of the discussion.

The air went out of me.

Dr. Foyer put my hand on his arm and guided me out. "Think it over. You'll see the wisdom of my advice." He squeezed my shoulder and left me bewildered in the middle of the hall.

I didn't remember walking back to my room. I remained numb as Chuck drove me home, though he kept up a running monologue. I was trying to clear my thoughts, to think. Unlike many people who grew more incisive when angry, I often grew more confused. My mind became gauze, and I couldn't draw any conclusions.

But as Chuck and I sped along the highway, I began to boil. My boss was spineless.

"Hey!" yelled Chuck, knocking on my head. "Anybody home?"

"Sorry," I said. "I'm just so mad I can hardly breathe." I explained what had happened with Ruth and Dr. Foyer.

"That's Foyer, all right," said Chuck, hitting the steering wheel. "Slimy as okra!"

The roar of cars passing, the swish of tires splattering puddles, the ticking of windshield wipers—all dimmed as the lid of the Fort Pitt Tunnel closed over us.

"So what are you going to do?" Chuck took my fingers in his bear-paw hand.

"I don't know. To defy Ruth openly will cause a huge rupture. But to pretend I'm doing as she wishes . . ." I pressed my free hand against my temples. "It's giving me a headache."

"Put your seat back and rest," he suggested. "We're hitting a traffic jam."

As the car rolled to a stop, Chuck leaned over, and I saw his sweater, colorful as Christmas wrap. He kissed me, a brief, skittering kiss. I was shocked, but, I had to admit, pleased. He was soft as moss, and sweet. My nose tickled with the smell of his shaving lotion, and the rest of me felt giddy. Rain beat on the roof of the car, and I heard music in it.

He wiggled my hand. "Want to have Thanksgiving dinner with the Tedeshis?"

I turned to him. "That's so nice, but Hannah invited me to her parents' home in Erie. We're leaving right after work tomorrow."

Chuck kissed me again at the Schenley Arms. "Sure you can't change your plans?"

I shook my head. "Sorry." I stepped out of his car, realizing that our friendship had been transformed. I smiled. Caterpillars to butterflies.

In the apartment I brewed tea, then went slack in the brown wingback chair, the leather still smelling of my grandfather's cigars. Chuck. I felt my face break into a grin. Never would I have expected Chuck, my pal . . . I sipped the tea and tried to recapture the feel of my hand in his, of his lips.

My stomach growled, and I went to the kitchen to heat up the leftover chicken I'd broiled last night. That was when the less pleasant part of the day came back to me. The Braille controversy. Whatever was I going to do about it?

As I ate, I considered Dr. Foyer's advice. But Ruth had all my students in other classes. Surely she would discover how far they had progressed in Braille.

I stood and flung a suitcase on my bed. I packed and kept trying to decide what to do, but I got nowhere.

I sighed and gave up thinking. I grabbed an apple and corrected Braille homework assignments. The headache returned, moving from my temples to the back of my head. I put away the work and took a hot bath. I still didn't know what to do about my Braille classes, but I listened to a record of *Newsweek*, choosing to worry about them in the morning.

❦ 11 ❧

But in the morning I had a more gripping worry. I awoke to the alarm and thought there must be a mistake. It couldn't be six-thirty yet. The room was shrouded in gray.

I jerked up, trembling, fumbling for the lamp. It clicked on, and I felt the warmth. I saw a hovering yellow glow, penetrating the haze, but nothing else. Nothing more distinct. I whirled and saw a rectangle of yellow light—the window. It glowed like a movie screen in a darkened theater—without characters, scenery, or action.

With frantic motions I shook my hand in front of my face. Yesterday I would have seen my elbow, my lower arm, my hand, blurry but recognizable. Now the air moved against my cheek, but I saw nothing. Nothing but gray mist.

I turned back to the lamp and window. Yes, I could distinguish light, but nothing else.

Dread crawled along my arms and neck and spine. My stomach clenched. Another hemorrhage. Oh, no, not a hemorrhage. This one would be irreversible, I was sure of it. I'd had so little sight left that any new bleeding would destroy it.

I tightened my hand into a fist, then jumped up and started to the bathroom. My shin slammed into the wretched coffee table. "Damn!" I yelled, and rubbed the throbbing bump.

I circled around the table and groped for the bathroom door. "Oh, God, I can't even function in my apartment now."

With shaking hands I held a warm washcloth over my eyes, my forehead.

"Oh, please, don't let this have happened," I prayed. "Not now. Not yet. Not ever."

My throat ached. Had what I feared finally happened? The death blow to my sight? Was I totally, completely blind? Was I left with only light perception? What possible good was that?

My ears blocked, and the floor seemed to tilt. I steadied myself against the sink and swallowed.

I wavered on a precipice, wanting to remove the cloth and test the left eye, wanting to keep the eye covered forever. My head, my stomach, my whole heart ached.

Finally, I withdrew the washcloth and leaned close to the mirror, desperate to see something. Anything. Color, form, movement. Anything in addition to light and dark.

Yet I saw nothing but light. Nothing.

❧ 12 ❧

The thing unspoken, the unspeakable, had finally happened.

I crumpled to the side of the tub, hugging myself, sinking into a hidden, secret place.

How long I sat, letting the weight bear down on me, I didn't know. Then the chill in the room, the cold porcelain penetrated, and I shivered back to consciousness.

I couldn't face work today; I would phone in sick. I'd curl up in bed, resting, letting the blood in the eye settle. But that wouldn't help me regain any sight! Besides, I had responsibilities. There weren't ready substitutes to teach Claire and Scott and Leon.

And Hannah—her parents were expecting me, preparing Thanksgiving dinner. I couldn't disappoint them now, so late.

I stood and fumbled for my toothbrush, holding it by the bristles as usual. The toothpaste coiled down my fingers and into the sink. I threw down the brush and swore, then placed the tube directly into my mouth and squeezed. I felt in the sink for the tooth-brush. Finally, I was able to brush.

I poured handfuls and handfuls of hot water over my face, still wishing the water, the heat, would lift the film from my eye.

But it didn't.

I made my way along the bare floor till I felt the rug, then trailed the wall to the closet. I groped from hanger to hanger, feeling each sweater, each pair of pants, each skirt. I tried to form a mental picture of the colors. My outfit had to match. I swore again. Why hadn't I labeled my clothes with Braille tags that showed color? Because I could always see the color—that was why.

I bit hard on my lip. So many clothes felt the same that I couldn't distinguish them. I threw myself at the clothes, ripping blouses, sweaters, skirts from the hangers, tossing them to the floor. Then I leaned against the remaining clothes, letting their softness and warmth soothe me.

Slowly I remembered that two pairs of pants were labeled—my navy and my black ones. Those colors had been too similar. I rummaged through the pile on the closet floor and found the black pants. I fumbled for a red sweater that I knew felt completely different from anything else. Finally, I could dress.

In the kitchen I spilled granola over the counter,

then heard it spray across the floor. As I poured tea, I burned my finger. I tossed the mug and cereal bowl into the sink without eating, pleased by the clatter, wanting to smash them and everything on my shelves. I ignored the cereal mess, pressed my hands to my face, and tried to control the trembling.

I was crazy with anger, crazy with fear, crazy with sadness. How was I going to pull this off? Sure, throughout my training I had used my other senses, wearing occluders, those stupid goggles with rubber where the plastic lenses should have been. But for more than three months I hadn't used them. Oh, God, I'd used that minuscule bit of sight for everything. Everything.

I searched for the chair and collapsed into it. I had to leave soon, meet Chuck downstairs, face the staircase, yawning, threatening.

And the guild—how would I negotiate that without any sight? Yesterday I could see legs and feet and stairs. Today I would see nothing. I'd swat everyone's ankles with my cane, careen into trainees, plunge down the basement stairs. What kind of role model was I going to be now?

What an impostor! What a fraud! Receiving praise for every step I'd taken. Applause for my courage. Before was nothing, now was everything. Now I would know challenge.

And I was so tired. I laid my head on the arm of the chair. "I can't do this."

But I had to do it. I had to go to work.

I dragged myself from the chair, picked up my cane and overnight bag, and started out. When I estimated that the stairs were a few feet away, I slowed and inched ahead. How could I find it now without plummeting from the top step?

Suddenly my cane dropped down. My heart dipped, too. With shaky hands I slid the cane to the right to find the handrail. I gripped it, teetering. Then I moved down the stairs like someone with a fierce hangover, methodical, cautious, as if each step sent waves of pain throbbing through my body.

Outside, the weather was cold and deadly calm. To me it looked the same as inside the building, only brighter—gray blending with gray, like a Newfoundland winter landscape. Sprinkles of snow brushed my cheeks. Oh, no, snow! More good luck! Blind person's fog, obstructing contact between my feet and the sidewalk. If we got enough of it, I'd have to slide along the stuff and attempt to distinguish between the street and sidewalk, the curb hidden by mounds of steel-hard snow.

Chuck pulled up in his Peugeot and beeped. I searched for the door handle. We rode along, he cheery with talk of the upcoming Steeler football game. I blessed the seat belt for holding me together.

Chuck must have noticed that I wasn't offering much to the conversation. He took my hand and squeezed it.

"So what's the verdict with Ruth—fight or flight?"

Ruth—oh, no! I'd completely forgotten.

Anger welled in me. Defiance. "Fight," I said, making up my mind in that instant. "War."

I sighed. Ruth. I'd have no patience with her today. Just getting through the building, through my classes, would make me battle-weary. If she provoked me in any way, I'd heap curses on her or burst into tears.

Chuck talked on, trying to draw me out. But his efforts were futile. I was so deeply consumed by my thoughts, so distraught, that I uttered a yes or no, nothing else. For miles, silence swelled between us.

"Sally, are you upset that I kissed you yesterday?" he asked finally.

I crawled from my cavern and turned to him. "No," I said, my voice not above a whisper. "No," I repeated. "Why?"

"You're so quiet," he said. "I just thought . . . well, it's not your style."

I took a deep breath. "I had a hemorrhage last night. Now all my sight is gone."

"God, Sally." He grabbed my hand again and rubbed it against his cheek, kissed it, then just held it tight. "I'm sorry."

I laid my forehead against his shoulder, cushioned by the down ski jacket. "It makes such a difference."

He swerved off the parkway, turned off the ramp, and stopped the car. He pulled me against his chest and, like a huge St. Bernard, hugged me. He comforted me the way I'd been comforted as a child.

After a while Chuck swung back onto the road. In the parking lot at the guild I mumbled a quick prayer. "Please, God, help."

I trudged off, tapping ahead of Chuck, who was dragging things from the car.

"Sal," he called. "Wrong way. Make a left."

I stopped, feeling the weight of the new, total blindness, seeing the gray go charcoal.

Chuck caught up to me. "Here," he said. "Latch on."

I took his arm. "I probably veered in the direction the earth turns," I said.

He laughed, but the joke went flat, and I climbed the stone steps to face responsibility.

Chuck guided me through the spacious lobby. Anything wide and long without reference boundaries could swallow me up now, confuse me.

"You're at the hallway to the Braille room," he whispered. "Hang in there."

I slapped my cane left and right, announcing to competitors that I was charging down the hall, too. Oh, I'd lost all grace. I slammed and thumped around like a beginner, rough, crude. Gone were the days of the nimble, lithe, quick, graceful movements, the movements of the water ballet star.

But I couldn't care about style, form, technique. All about me were amorphous dangers—objects to hit me, holes to fall into. Now with every step I risked injury, death, or worse—absurdity.

I made it through the day, sealed up in my room. The bathroom was down the hall, first door on the left, and I ventured no farther. Chuck and Hannah brought me lunch. To them, I must have looked like an awakened corpse. Well, part of me *was* a corpse— two corpses: my eyes, entombed in a living body. A body willing and wanting to do well, work well, move at twice its speed.

At five o'clock Chuck closed the door to my Braille room and kissed and kissed me. "Any run-ins with Ruth?" he asked.

I sighed. "No, thank heaven."

"Call me," he said. "You going to be okay?"

"Yes," I promised.

But I wasn't.

Hannah's parents couldn't have been lovelier, but they were strangers, and their house was unfamiliar. The newness, unfortunately, only aggravated the tension. I could barely interact. At Thanksgiving dinner, I ate the mashed potatoes easily, but the turkey, the whole stems of broccoli, the Jell-O salad evaded me.

"May I cut your meat?" Hannah asked quietly.

"No, thanks," I said. Somehow I preferred starving to getting help. I'd been able to cut anything, eat everything before. I endured the dinner without eating, without speaking—stricken.

After dinner, in the bedroom, Hannah spoke. "Sally, before this hemorrhage, could you see your food?"

I shook my head. The vision had been too blurry to distinguish much on the plate. So Hannah's point was on target. My inability to eat was all psychological. Probably my whole reaction was psychological. But I couldn't care. I just wanted to be home, in solitude, healing my psyche, not struggling to be charming.

As soon as possible, I phoned Chuck. "I couldn't eat anything," I blurted out. "Everything on my plate felt like small granite sculptures."

He laughed. "Told you that you should have come to the Tedeshis'. We served only finger food. Turkey, veggies, the works on toothpicks." The teasing helped.

And the next day I got home, burrowed into bed, and closed my eyes. With eyes closed, I could pretend that there had been no change in my health.

But Monday morning arrived, and with it came harsh reality. Like it or not, I had to greet it.

~❧ 13 ❧~

Snow had fallen overnight, was still falling—huge, limp, wet drops. The sidewalk, the solid structure that gave definition to my world, lay buried under snow —about six inches' worth. Cars crawled along Bigelow Boulevard, wipers clicking. Tires spun and whined up Centre Avenue.

Chuck would never make it up the hill to the Schenley Arms. Without thinking, I stepped off the porch, determined to meet him at the bottom. Snowflakes, like damp feathers, brushed my cheeks as I tramped along. The snow actually did blanket everything, quiet everything except for the spinning, frantic tires and revving engines.

I touched, then dug, the tip of my cane left and right, feeling for concrete underneath. But the accumulation was too deep, maybe *more* than six inches. Did the guild call off school? I didn't think so.

I couldn't feel the lawn in front of the building. I pushed my cane tip to the right—no boundary there either. The curb snow merged with the street snow and hid all my tactile clues.

I swallowed. Maybe I shouldn't have ventured off

the porch. Not this way, without the travel vision I'd had six days ago. I'd stepped from the porch on impulse, forgetting that I'd lost everything.

I turned back, but I wasn't sure now where the porch was. I spun around one hundred and eighty degrees.

I *would* pick a day like today to be a hero! Well, my ears might help. I took aim at the screaming tires and, with mounting misgivings, forged ahead.

The path underfoot sloped down, and I followed it left. Downhill. This must be the way to Craig and Centre. The tires spun and gnawed at the road behind me. Surely this direction was right. I relaxed my shoulders and flexed my fingers in the gloves. I shook my head, spilling snow from my hair down my neck. Wouldn't I surprise Chuck!

The wind picked up, spraying snow like grains of sand. I pulled my collar closer about me. No cars crept past. Buildings muffled the tire sounds behind me, and the sidewalk, or what I thought was sidewalk, leveled off. My stomach knotted, and I clenched my free hand into a fist. Something was very wrong.

I stopped and tried to keep from becoming rattled. What would Gail Zimmerman tell me to do? Listen. The cars' tires and engines, my only sound cues, were behind me, but not directly behind. I'd strayed to the right of them somehow.

I whirled and trudged back, hoping to put myself

right below the car sounds, my friends. "Feel," I commanded. "With cane, with feet." Talking to myself kept the panic at bay, but it was there, pressing. The ground sloped upward, crested, then sloped downward. That was the way a street felt, not a sidewalk. Was I crossing a street, then? I stepped onto a level surface. Damn this weather! Snow everywhere, concealing every bit of information I needed. And I hadn't dressed for arctic weather. I was growing numb bit by bit, fingertips, toes.

I stood still, turned my head left and right, straining for sounds—cars, passersby. Where were the pedestrians, anyway? Where was Chuck? What a day for him to be late! My heart beat louder than a metronome.

Calm down, I ordered myself. Think. I had to unravel the jumble. Gail would make me consider the different scenarios. But my mind whirled like the tires. Blood surged through my head, and my breath came fast. I was losing the battle against panic.

Then somebody's arms were around me, squeezing me, pulling me against his wet face for a kiss. "Hey," said Chuck, laughing, "what are you doing down here? I was about to put an All Points Bulletin out on you."

I couldn't laugh. I couldn't speak.

"Why'd you come to Dithridge and Centre?"

"Good day for a stroll," I said.

He guided me uphill to his warm car, and I collapsed into it. The wonderful Peugeot skidded and spurted along the city streets, then the parkway. Chuck parked, led me, and I entered the guild shell-shocked, but forcing a smile. He dropped me at the hallway to my office.

In the Braille room, I took the first seat and tried to pull myself together. My classes, students, dissolved into a sea of voices, indistinguishable from one another. Somehow I made it through the morning.

At lunchtime, I finished working with Leon, then sat at my desk correcting papers. Footsteps clattered toward my door.

"Sally."

I flinched at the sound of Dr. Foyer's voice. Were there more repercussions from the Braille dispute? So far, I'd managed to avoid Ruth. Hiding helped.

"I've had sandwiches sent to my office," he said. "I saw you in the lobby this morning and decided to speak to you over lunch."

He'd seen me? Staggering through the lobby? Leaning heavily on Chuck? I would rather talk about the Braille problem.

I searched for my cane, felt around in a circle, and found dust balls, air, nothing more.

"Farther right, honey," he said.

Softness, sympathy, could make me crack.

Dr. Foyer guided me upstairs to his office. He led me to the chair I'd occupied during our odious last meeting. Then he closed the door.

"Are you falling apart on me, Sally?" he asked, settling into his desk chair.

"No," I said with more resolution than I felt.

"You've had four months of cane training with your eyes occluded. Why are you having so much trouble adjusting to the total blindness?"

It was that obvious, then? Visible to the whole outside world? My smile hadn't camouflaged the pain. Or had Chuck told him? No. Dr. Foyer had just witnessed the difference in me.

I tried to speak, but the words stuck in my throat. I shook my head, waved my hand.

"You're a big girl, Sally. I thought you were tougher than this."

"It hurts," I snapped. "It's a big loss."

He placed a box of tissues on my lap. "Yes, it is, honey."

I laid my head on my arm and cried.

When I finished, I leaned against the back of the chair.

"Want a sandwich?" he asked.

I shook my head. "I want mobility," I said. "Around the building and outside. It won't take much to get my confidence back."

"That's my girl," Dr. Foyer said.

"I could ask Chuck or Gail—"

He interrupted. "You shouldn't ask your friends. Friendship and business don't mix."

I sighed. He was right. And right about more than just not employing my friends. He was doing me a favor. He was making me face reality and begin coping, much sooner than I would have on my own.

I dabbed my face with a tissue. Maybe he wasn't such a villain, after all. He'd been slippery about the Braille conflict. But he'd helped me today, and I was grateful.

"I can hook you up with one of our community mobility specialists," he said.

"How much?" I asked flatly. With my seven-thousand-dollar salary and plans to save for graduate school, money was always an issue. But I had no choice.

"Five dollars an hour," said Dr. Foyer.

"Sold," I said, standing. I aimed for his door and thumped forward, hitting a wall with my cane.

"Six inches left, Sally," he directed.

The next day re-mobility began. The community mobility specialist, Roger, came during lunch and reviewed the building with me. In an hour I'd put the sound and tactile clues back together: hum of the soda machine by the dining room, carpet in the lobby, dip in the hall floor to my office. He even made me listen for the clink of my cane on the metal strip announcing the basement staircase so that I could avoid an imprudent plunge.

After three weeks and ten lessons, I'd regained the lost confidence. I wanted more lessons, just for orientation purposes, but my funds were scarce, especially with Christmas just a few days away. Still, I decided to meet with Roger a few more times after the holidays. I'd think of it as a present to myself.

❧14❧

The day before Christmas break I entered the Braille room and began to arrange my papers, my ritual start to the workday. My suitcase was packed and under my desk, and I was eager for vacation, for my trip home to Conyngham.

A throat cleared, and I jerked around, knocking over my purse. "Oh," I cried, "you startled me!" My whole body tingled with surprise.

The person didn't identify himself, didn't emit a sound. My heart lunged against my chest, and the floor seemed to move. "Did you want something?" I asked, hoping it wasn't my purse, my life.

Still no answer. I gripped the chair, my blood pounding. Was I in danger? With sight, I could have sized up the situation quickly. But now . . .

Low, muffled sobs broke the silence, and I rushed to the sound. Someone, a woman, fell against me and wept. "Oh, Miss Hobart!"

"Claire?"

Her head nodded against me. "Oh, honey, what is it?"

She was crying too hard to speak, with quivering, convulsive sobs. I waited, stroking her hair, holding her.

When she stopped crying, I moved away to close the door and bring her tissues.

"What is it, Claire?" I repeated, still keeping an arm around her.

She trembled, fought more tears, then heaved a huge sigh. "The night supervisor, ah, she found Richard and me in a parked car, kissing." She shuddered.

Richard? Who was that? Then it hit me—Dr. Allen. My star pupil. Married. A dozen years older than Claire.

I drew up a chair beside her. "What did the night supervisor do?"

Claire's shoulders straightened. "Phoned Dr. Foyer. And he's just been yelling at me. If this hadn't been our last day, Dr. Foyer would have kicked us out."

Kick them out? I couldn't condone an illicit relationship, but it was not exactly a crime, and it wasn't unusual for the trainees to fall in love. When I was a trainee, love blossomed over and over again among my friends. But the staff always knew, probably intervened when the relationships seemed inappropriate. Privacy, taken for granted by most sighted people, was rare. The blind lived in a fishbowl here.

I asked, "Have you spoken to your counselor about your feelings for Richard?"

She waved her hand, accidentally hitting my arm. "No. I can't talk to him."

I lifted her chin. "Do you love Richard?"

She nodded. "And he loves me. He's going to get a divorce."

I sighed. Maybe. But the cynic in me thought this hope was folly.

Double knocks beat on my door. "Anybody there?" Scott's and Lou's voices.

I stood. "Just a minute," I called.

Claire didn't react, just continued her story as if her ears were impaired, too. "And now Eddie wants to fight Richard."

I frowned. "Eddie?"

"Yes," she said. "He and I met in the hospital. He's been jealous . . ."

Ah, now I understood Eddie's behavior toward Dr. Allen.

More knocks. "Hey, Miss H. You in there?"

I hurried to the door. "Come back in ten minutes, guys. Okay?"

I went back to Claire and sat down. "Will you speak to my old counselor, Emily Feldstein?" I asked. "She's easy to talk to and, I think, really helpful."

Claire stood, and I took her to Emily. Blindness—it pulled the foundation out from under a person. Stripped her of confidence, self-esteem. If Claire found someone to love her, then she'd feel restored, worthwhile. Angry as I was at Richard Allen, I knew that the same was true of him. Blindness had dealt its blow. If a woman was attracted to him again, he would feel valued and valuable.

I couldn't put Claire and Richard out of my mind. As I'd hugged her goodbye outside of Emily's office, I asked, "You going to be all right?"

"Fine," she said and whispered, "I'll invite you to the wedding."

I wasn't as optimistic as Claire, and I walked back to the Braille room feeling slightly depressed.

"You going to give a broken-down old bachelor a hug for the road, Miss H.?"

Scott startled me. "No, but I'll give *you* one."

Our canes collided as he gave me a brisk squeeze.

"You *are* taller than Jackie Kennedy," he declared. I laughed.

"By the way, Lou had to leave. He said to tell you goodbye."

Then Scott's fingers brushed my cheek, my nose, lips, eyes, hair.

Ruth Becher would have hit the ceiling if she'd witnessed this professional slip, but I didn't care.

"I'll miss you, teach," he said hoarsely.

"Me too, Scott. Good luck."

I walked down the hall to say goodbye to Eddie, Richard Allen, and the other trainees.

On the nine-hour bus ride to Conyngham, I thought about Scott and his ex-wife, about Richard and Claire, about Chuck and myself. Did we all need the affirmation of another to feel complete, restored? Was a meaningful relationship the only thing that gave people peace and contentment?

Christmas arrived with a great wind, tricking us into expecting snow. None came.

My brother, Bobby, returned from Vietnam. His hug was that of the same large, rambling brother I'd known, but it was thinner, quicker, more tense. The war had taken its toll.

My parents welcomed him back with an enormous party. My sister, Marti, her husband, Larry, and their trio, Tracy, Erik, and squirt Amy, arrived from Michigan. Chuck also made the trip.

Just before the guests appeared, Daddy gathered me against his barrel tummy and hugged me for a long time. The smell of Old Spice and eggnog mingled with the pine tree—Christmas.

"Know what I like about you?" Daddy asked the question I'd been hearing for twenty-six years.

I nodded.

"Everything," he said. "Know what I don't like about you?"

I smiled, knowing this answer, too.

"Nothing," he said, kissing my hair. "Now that I've got you home," he continued, "I'm not letting you go."

I smiled and smooched him. To stay there in that warm holiday spot was tempting. But I remembered the poem of the snowman, pitied by the boy for being out in the cold world. He wanted to bring the snowman into his warm home. But he couldn't. The snowman would melt.

I stayed in the safety and protection of that cozy home for a week. Then I returned to Pittsburgh to keep from melting.

A new group of trainees arrived. I missed Scott and Lou and Claire. But Leon returned for fifteen more weeks, and I was happy. Happy, that is, when the

shadow of Ruth Becher didn't fall on me. I had continued to teach as if there had been no disagreement
over the Braille instruction.

Yet with each week, Ruth's animosity seemed to
grow. If another staff member whispered to me in a
meeting, Ruth hushed me. If I offered a suggestion,
she found reason to disapprove. The treatment made
me defensive, gave me pangs, but I resolved to do my
best work and ignore her. My goal was still to work
long enough to save for graduate school in English,
and I couldn't let Ruth interfere.

But during the second week in January, she
marched into the Braille room. "Do you intend to
ignore my wishes again this session?" she asked
haughtily.

"I don't ignore them, exactly. I wish we could
reconcile—" I began.

"I insist that you teach the Braille my way," she
interrupted. "Every single student must have Grade
One and Grade Two Braille."

I leaned back against my desk. "I'm sorry, Ruth. I
just cannot in good conscience." My cheeks burned.

"But don't you see—" She slapped a tabletop.
"Why do I talk to you—headstrong, stubborn girl!"
She stormed out to the hall. "You'll regret this," she
hissed. "Mark my words."

I dropped into my chair, only then beginning to

tremble. For the rest of the week I prepared for reprisals, but none came. She spoke as little as possible to me, but never again brought up the dispute.

For diversion, I enrolled in a Shakespeare class that met one evening a week at the University of Pittsburgh. The course did bring novelty to my schedule and almost total delight.

Almost. On my way back from class one night, a man called to me and snatched my arm. "I'll help you," he offered. His breath was a brewery, and I began to feel frightened. I was no longer a sprinter, able to make swift escapes. But I pulled away, adrenaline-charged, and actually did run across the street. Better to run on a street than a sidewalk with edges and curbs to fall from.

The man followed, calling after me, telling me to slow down.

I escaped that night. It was my good luck that the man had filled himself so full of grog. But the experience scared me. I was easy prey for muggers and worse. From then on, I walked home with a married man from the class who also lived at the Schenley Arms.

The other evenings I spent with Chuck, grading Braille papers, listening to TV. He was easy to be with. Always fair weather; no storms, as there'd been with Tom. I told Chuck I loved him, and I wanted to mean it. He lifted the burdens, soothed, and never hurt me. Wasn't love possible without wrenchings and wounds? Surely. But was what I felt for Chuck love?

❧ 15 ❧

January and February tried my patience with beating winds and freezing rains. Any snow that fell hardened into jagged mounds, treacherous to the blind traveler. Even March offered no break in the weather. I slogged through the nipping, gnawing cold, going out as little as possible—to and from my Shakespeare class, my newfound church.

Chuck was the one warm spot in the winter. We were always together. He still drove me back and forth to work, often picking up things for me at stores. I took the bus only two times a week, on Chuck's and my afternoons off.

One day I searched for him between classes.

"Did Chuck leave already?" I asked, poking my head into the faculty lounge.

"Yes," said Emily. "You were tied up, and he didn't want to interrupt."

"Shoot," I said. "I wanted him to drop off a sweater at the cleaner for me."

Emily came up to me then. "Why can't you do that yourself, Sally?"

Caught, I felt chagrined from brow to toe. "I get your point," I managed to say. "It's embarrassing, but you're right."

I thumped back to class, miserable, realizing that I'd been leaning too heavily on Chuck. Yet hadn't he been willing? Hadn't he offered? Yes. I should have resisted, though. The dry cleaner was fifteen blocks away, without pickup and delivery. Too far to walk, at least in this weather. I would just have to take a cab.

I greeted my visualization class and tried to focus on the lesson. "Stories abound," I began, "of sailors guiding their boats through deep fog. They smell the smoke from the chimneys of the houses along the banks. They call out and hear their voices bounce off the cliffs. They hear the water rush across rocks and up against the shore. With their ears, their noses, they form pictures and navigate to safety.

"Blindness takes away the world around you. When you first became blind or at any time after, did you panic because of this lost world? Because you were connected only by your feet to the floor?"

"Yes," they chorused.

"You can hear the knocking of the radiator, feel a wall, or smell the coffee in the pot. You can also visualize these things.

"Today Miss Howard and I are joining forces to show you how your senses, combined with your ability to visualize, can help you connect to your environment and navigate the streets of your neighborhoods."

Teaching reassured me. I was not a worthless parasite.

But on the two buses home, I was as lost as the sailor in the fog. Preoccupied. Any disabled person could fall into the same trap—having a loved one doing too much for her. How much did a person do for another out of love, and how much did he do out of obligation? Was Chuck trying to foster dependence? No, not Chuck.

When he came over after dinner, I asked him how he felt.

"So far I haven't minded picking up stuff for you," he said, stretching back on the couch. "But sometimes I wonder if you really love me, or if you just need me to make your life easier."

I sighed. Love or need? Which was it? I hadn't thought about it for a long time, and I still wasn't sure. I sensed Chuck's wish for reassurance. He leaned toward me, waiting, wanting an answer. Guilt tugged like an undertow. I owed him the truth, not just a hasty response to put him at ease. But what was the truth?

He sat back. "You haven't met thousands of men since going blind. Now and then I think you're just hanging on to me till someone better comes along."

"No, honestly, I'm not doing that," I protested. "I have no interest in meeting anybody else." That was true. Chuck contented me, never bored me. In that way he was like Brian or Carol, my best friends. So was that what our relationship was, then—friendship?

This thought confused me, and I fell silent. My mind was a maze of doubts.

Somehow we strayed to other topics, listened to TV, and parted as if nothing had changed. But the conversation had driven a wedge between us.

Before long, Chuck became less available. He met someone else and began to date her, still reserving one weekend night for me. I missed him and felt jealous pangs, but had no right. Sometime in April we stopped dating, stopped riding to work together.

I decided to retire from the romantic field altogether. It had been only a year since the broken engagement with Tom; maybe I didn't have the capacity to love another man yet. Meanwhile, I had friends, a marvelous family, work. I was building a life.

Romance was just one of my goals, and it could wait.

I concentrated on my female friends, Gail, Hannah, Emily, my new church friend Rachel, and work.

But work was not all triumph either, although my students and classes were wonderful. Leon continued to progress, greeting me each day with a new word he'd learned.

"S-a-l-u-t-a-tion sign-s, Miss H."

He buoyed my spirits, but the dreary fight with Ruth, now a cold standoff, was wearing. Although all my other colleagues were supportive, her hostility chilled the otherwise warm atmosphere.

Early in May she made good on her threat. Her penalty came in the form of the most minimal raise in my contract for the coming fiscal year.

"One hundred dollars? That's my raise?" I asked in disbelief.

Her victory was palpable. "If it were up to me, I would deny you any raise whatsoever!"

I walked out of her office, struggling with pride and principle and visions of poverty. Still, I pressed on, determined to do my work well. I aspired to be like medieval carvers who sculpted the undersides of choir seats. Their goal was to do something not for public praise but for their own satisfaction.

And on work breaks, when I wasn't socializing

with Gail, Emily, or Hannah, I started listening to one of the Shakespeare plays on my reading list.

One afternoon, while I was in the middle of *As You Like It*, Dr. Foyer interrupted. "On breaks you should be reading in your profession," he said, "not reading for pleasure."

I thought of Chuck and his friends reading *Sports Illustrated*, and frowned. But I punched off the tape recorder and pulled out Braille homework to correct.

A few weeks later, Dr. Foyer rebuked me again. In meetings, other staff members doodled. They passed their drawings from one to another, writing and whispering comments. Chuck used to describe the funniest cartoons to me. Through it all, I knitted and purled.

"Sally, please put away the knitting," said Dr. Foyer in the middle of one meeting. "I know you need to count two knits, two purls, and you can't concentrate fully on the meeting."

I complied, but stung with outrage. My knitting was not so demanding. I knitted one row, then purled the next. Simple. Little concentration required. Certainly less than for doodling.

But I had to admit that the doodlers must be less conspicuous. They could appear to be taking notes; I probably stuck out like a huge knitting needle.

Furthermore, I was glad that Dr. Foyer didn't

withhold his punches because I was blind. I grew to appreciate his respect, even if it manifested itself in a rebuke.

Spring gave way to summer. I stretched my legs freely, walked among birdsong, enjoyed all sounds, all tones. I went out on Friday nights with Emily and her husband, and other colleagues, and had a few dates with a sidekick of Arnie's. My church friend, Rachel, owned some woods north of Pittsburgh. She and I camped and hiked, even swam in the Clarion River, which abutted her property.

I worked, saved money, and prepared final reports on my students. Soon Leon would leave and enroll at the Vocational Rehabilitation Center, the VRC. I wrote an elaborate outline of the reading work we'd covered and proposed further study. My report was lengthy, but clear and thorough. I expected someone at the VRC to pick up where I'd left off with Leon.

On the last day before the guild closed for vacation, Dr. Foyer summoned me to his office again. I entered with none of the dread I'd had on former visits, and took a seat.

"Sally," he began, "the report you wrote about Leon . . ."

I nodded, anticipating praise despite my alliance with the medieval carvers.

"Well, I'm not sending that along to the VRC."

I frowned. "Why not? Even if there are no reading specialists, someone could follow my outline and nudge him along. Without it, I'm afraid Leon could slide back."

"Inventions, ideas generated by a member of a company are company property, honey. What you've designed for Leon is guild property, and I'm not sharing it."

His words absolutely dumbfounded me. "What's in that outline is basic phonics. I designed nothing."

"I read it, Sally. Don't sell yourself short."

I wanted to scream. I shook my head, tried to clear it. "But this way Leon suffers." Tears were tripping me up.

"It's not the way you learned it in Sunday school, honey," he said. "But that's my decision." He stood and offered me his arm.

I ignored his arm and stormed out. It was not the smoothest dramatic exit. But I banged my cane in ferocious protest all the way down the hall.

In the Braille room, I squeezed both hands into fists. I would quit. Even though the guild had taught me so much, had given me confidence. I just couldn't work for a man who would sacrifice his students' best interests.

When I finished my last class, I asked Leon to stay

behind. I Brailled my telephone number and handed it to him. "Call me if you need anything."

"No joke?" he asked.

I smiled. "Even if you just want to talk. Take it from me, there might be some rough days."

He tapped to the door, then stopped. "Miss H.?"

"Yes, Leon?"

He paused. "You're a great teacher. Thanks."

I swallowed. "Good luck, Leon."

I grabbed my things, walked to Dr. Foyer's office, and submitted my resignation.

"Hold on, honey," Dr. Foyer called. "Don't throw a tantrum."

I kept walking.

He caught up to me. "Sally, I don't want to lose you."

I turned. "Then send the material to the VRC."

"No can do," he said.

I tapped away and hurried down the steps.

"Hobart!" Gail followed me out the front door. "What's going on? Emily overheard you and Foyer. You really quitting?"

I nodded.

"No offense, Sal . . ." It was Emily. "But what are you going to do for money?"

I waved my hand. "Mooch off you," I said, hugging her, then Gail.

But Emily's question haunted me all the way home. I was determined not to fall back on my parents. I had enough money for a few months. Combined with righteous indignation and faith, it would have to support me somehow.

Part Two

16

September 1970

Had I been reckless in quitting my job? Would I be penniless at the end of the year and forced to limp back to my parents? I hoped not.

I entered the University of Pittsburgh, signing up for four English courses: seventeenth- and eighteenth-century British literature, medieval literature, and a nineteenth-century novels class. My goal was to do well enough in these four courses to earn a teaching assistantship by January 1971, when my savings would run out.

Through the Library of Congress, I obtained most of the required books on the syllabi, either on records or on reel-to-reel tapes. For the books and other materials that were not recorded, I needed to find readers. The State Office for the Blind would reimburse me for such services, so I put up ads and hired two women about my age. Also, one of the Pittsburgh synagogues offered volunteer reading services, and two lovely women, jewels, signed up to help me each week.

I hired Roger, the community mobility specialist, to

orient me to the daunting Cathedral of Learning, the main classroom building on the campus. This tall structure was notorious for its deadly revolving doors and confusing elevators, which challenged even the sighted public.

Then classes began. I tapped down the six long blocks to the university, trembling, feeling the color rush to my face. I found the medieval literature class-room and dropped into the first seat that my cane whacked. Fortunately, no one else had taken it first. Right away, the professor launched into a lecture about Beowulf, great hero and slayer of the monster Grendel.

In the second class, eighteenth-century British lit., I was introduced to Samuel Johnson and grew curious about his dictionary and essays.

Afterward I made my way outside with contented thoughts. I located a sunny, grassy plot and sat down. Words, ideas—such pleasure. This occupation would be all sweetness.

With an hour before my next class I shoved my purse under my head and sunbathed. I was hungry, but didn't know where a snack bar was. I would have to eat lunch when I got home. In a few minutes a shadow fell over me.

"Hi," a man said. His voice was aimed my way. "We have the same English classes."

I stretched out my hand, reluctant to lose the solitude. Wary. I didn't want any flirtations.

"I'm Sally."

"Ira," he said, shaking my hand. He flopped down beside me. "My wife and I have seen you walking around Oakland, traveling on the bus."

His wife. Good. An insurance policy against romantic entanglement.

"We have a bet on about you," he continued.

My mouth dropped open. "A bet? Whatever for?"

"My wife thinks you are really blind, but I think you are wearing opaque contact lenses for an experiment."

I laughed. "Your wife wins; I'm really blind. I can only see light and dark."

"I'm straightforward," he said.

I smiled. "Yes, you are."

Ira had the same four courses, it turned out, and he, too, was after a teaching assistantship. We talked until it was time for our nineteenth-century novels class, where we learned about Jane Austen's heroine Emma. I left class, eager to begin the books.

Ira stopped me in the hall. "Do you want to have a beer? My wife should be done teaching soon," he said. "Maybe she can meet us."

I nodded, and we walked two blocks to the Craig Street Inn, Emily's husband's favorite bar.

"By the way, d-do you drink?" he stammered.

I had to grin. "Not heavily, but now and then."

I took his arm and asked him to guide me to a seat. We sat on stools at the counter.

"I had this notion that blind people were always virtuous," he said.

I laughed. "Well, I've disproved that."

Then someone yelled, "Sally! Hi, beautiful."

It was the bartender, Jimmy, Emily's friend. He took my hand and kissed me.

"What can I get you?" he asked.

"Whatever you have on draft," I said.

"Me too," said Ira.

After Jimmy set down our beers, Ira leaned toward me. "How do you know that guy so well?"

I leaned forward, too. Conspiring. "We're married," I whispered.

Ira didn't utter a word, so I laughed.

"Just kidding. He's a friend of my good friend."

Ira hit the counter. "That's why you're different," he said. "Blind people aren't supposed to have a sense of humor."

I frowned. "Virtuous and humorless. Blind people don't sound very appealing."

"Well, those are the stereotypes," he said. He clunked down his mug. "Be right back. I'm going to call my wife."

Ira came back, and we began to discuss the books,

the professors. Ira didn't just listen out of duty until he could impart his point. He listened sincerely, hung on to a subject, spoke with energy. He was refreshing, and so was his wife, Ilene, who joined us shortly after he called her.

They offered me a ride, but the weather was beautiful, and I chose to meander home by myself. Twenty minutes later, I started listening to *Emma*.

For days I read delightedly, thinking I'd found a green spot in the desert. This wasn't work; this was a holiday.

I began to miss Claire, Scott, Leon, all my students, and the teaching less. Claire wrote that she had heard nothing from Richard Allen. She put a good face on it, but I knew she was crushed. She hoped to enter college in January. College would help her to put Richard behind her.

Scott wrote. He was wrestling with his state office counselor over job retraining. I smiled. He would do well. But Leon—I heard nothing from him.

Around this time, though, four weeks into the semester, I hit my own obstacles. The quantity of reading and research proved too time-consuming. All my readers were excellent and reliable. None, however, was familiar with basic library procedures, and I was no pro either. At Bucknell I'd never taken courses that required lengthy research papers. Even with direction from the University of Pittsburgh's librarians, we spent most of my two-hour reading sessions searching for books. When we finally had them in hand, my readers had fifteen or twenty minutes remaining to read.

Another frustration was mechanical failure: typewriters, tape players. Records were often too scratchy to understand.

Still another problem was the university's lack of any system for dealing with the blind. My professors didn't even know how to give me tests. I offered to bring a typewriter and reader and asked only that they provide me with an empty room for taking a test. But none could ever find an empty room. I took the tests in nearby ladies' lavatories, trying to concentrate while women came in and out, flushing toilets, discussing dates.

All these frustrations forced me to make an unpleasant decision, to drop one of my courses. Since I cared the least about poetry, I chose to drop the seventeenth-century class. I'd quit my job at the guild for a good reason. I hated quitting this class because I couldn't handle the work load, blind. I worried that I'd lose all hope of an assistantship now and any means of further study or independent living.

But within a week I experienced a much greater concern, more threatening than financial dependence. My health, again, began to desert me.

❦ 17 ❦

"How long have you been hard-of-hearing, Miss Hobart?" asked Dr. Stanziola, entering the examining room.

Hard-of-hearing? What was the man talking about? He meant blind, didn't he?

The room was dense and quiet, except for the rain pinging the window, a child crying next door. My heart surged in my chest, and past slithered into present. I was back in time two years, in the office of my ophthalmologist, Dr. Taggart. The rickety stool squeaking under his weight. The lit cigarette sending smoke around his face. His serious, sad expression.

"What the hell happened to your eyes?" he'd asked.

I swallowed. My thoughts floated back to the present, to Dr. Stanziola, who'd just dealt the same kind of blow. "So the reduced hearing is not something simple like wax clogging the ear?" I asked.

"You didn't know?" Dr. Stanziola asked.

I shook my head, not trusting my voice.

"Well, it's a mild loss, primarily in the right ear—

nothing to interfere with much functioning." He patted my hand. "You might have a little more trouble hearing in crowded restaurants, anyplace that has excess background noise."

Oh, please. I raised the back of my hand to my mouth.

"Miss Hobart, are you all right?"

No, I wasn't. Blind people needed every decibel of sound.

I bit my lip to get control. "What could have caused it?" I asked. "When my hearing was checked at the guild a year and a half ago, it was perfect." This couldn't be happening.

"My secretary is phoning for your records," he said, rustling papers. "You said in the medical history that your father has some hearing loss."

I nodded, picturing Daddy cupping his ear to hear above the din of a crowded party.

"It's probably an inherited weakness, but we'll check into it."

I took a deep breath. The office smelled of stained wood, leather. Outside the room, the wind gusted and whined. I couldn't go through this again. "Are you going to run other tests?" Desperation—I heard it.

He stood. "Not right away. My secretary will make an appointment for you in two months. We'll conduct another hearing test then and see if there are any changes." He opened the door.

I was chasing him away. Too much need, pain. But I couldn't stop. "Is there medicine?"

"I want you to have histamine shots," he said. "My nurse will explain, and she'll guide you out."

Histamine? What for?

The door closed, and I sat in the examining chair, stunned. Was this really happening? My ears. My link to people, to independence. Something was wrong with my ears, and this doctor acted as if he were treating a common cold.

I wanted to run after him and shout, "I am blind. I cannot function without my hearing." But I was always the good patient. I just laid my head back and fought the tears.

For a week I'd been dizzy. Standing on a street corner, on a top step, I pitched forward or backward, catching myself before I fell. And then one evening, on the phone with Rachel, I'd switched the receiver from my left to my right ear and couldn't hear as well.

The dizziness had been easy to dismiss—flu, lack of sleep, stress. But the diminished hearing was so frightening that I scrambled for a doctor. The search had led me to Dr. Stanziola, one of the best ear doctors in the city. Best? Maybe. But rushed, insensitive.

His nurse entered the room and gave me a histamine shot. "What's this for?" I asked.

"To cure the dizziness."

She handed me an appointment card, then guided me out. I tapped down the sidewalk, numb, nearly oblivious, until I came to the corner and the transit stop.

On the bus home, I tried to put the hearing problem out of my mind. I had two tests and a paper to worry about. Dr. Stanziola had said it was a mild hearing loss, unlikely to cause trouble. But couldn't that have been said of my first hemorrhage—mild bleeding, not likely to cause much damage to the eye? Again I slid back two years to the eye clinic. Eye patches. Laser treatments. Reassurance from doctors.

Was I destined to lose my hearing, little by little, the way I'd lost my sight? No. That would be too much . . .

At home I tried to immerse myself in the concerns of Dorothea, heroine of *Middlemarch*, in the foibles of the pilgrims of *The Canterbury Tales*. But the books couldn't hold my attention. The fear, the dread, gained on me. What would be left? What pleasures? What reason to keep putting one foot in front of the other?

I dragged myself to class, studied, took tests, but my heart wasn't in it. My ears were all I could think about.

Somehow, keeping up the rhythm of routine, I got through the next month. The dizziness went away, and the hearing seemed no worse. I began to worry less.

At least about my ears. A new concern emerged, though.

"You got a B, Sally," announced Ira, looking at the grade on my term paper.

I slapped the desktop.

He batted me on the head with his paper—an A, as usual. "Don't be so hard on yourself. Remember what you've been going through." He shoved his elbow into my side. "Grab on. You can be a hero and walk by yourself tomorrow."

I sighed. "I have to face it, Ira. Original, analytical thinking is not my specialty. I'll never land a teaching assistantship now."

"It's the library hassles," he said. "I'll start helping you there."

"It's hopeless," I said. "I've been talking to Rachel . . ."

"The social worker?"

I nodded. "I've been exploring that master's program."

Ira stopped. "Then who am I going to talk to?"

I forced a smile. "I'll still be on campus."

But I wasn't even sure of that. I couldn't enroll in the graduate school of social work in January; I would have to wait until September. No matter what program I entered, I'd have to work part time to pay tuition and living costs. Where would I find a job? My possibilities were sorely limited—no waitressing, no clerking in stores. What could I do?

Just before Thanksgiving, Carol phoned. Her voice was sunshine. True to her nature, she questioned me and sought all my news.

I decided to spare her the hearing troubles until I'd had my second audiogram.

"Basically, I'm not cut out for an English Ph.D.," I said. "I have this friend who's a social worker. Well, I'm looking into that. It might suit me better, and I could work with kids."

"Sounds good," she said.

"So enough about me. How are you?"

"Fine," she said. "Mike and I are getting married." Understated, quiet as ever.

"Oh, that's wonderful," I said, tears stinging my eyes. "When?"

"Tomorrow," she said. "Neither of us wants a fuss, so we're going to a justice of the peace."

That was so like Carol—nothing showy. Keep it simple.

"Oh, Carol, I'm so happy for you. Mike sounds like a terrific guy." I pulled out the tail of my blouse and wiped my eyes. "I'm sure he deserves you."

"Thanks, Sal," she said.

Any minute she would realize that I was crying. "I don't want you to have a big phone bill," I said. "I'll call you in a few weeks. Love you, Carol."

"Love you, too," she said, and hung up.

I was thrilled for Carol. So why the tears?

I rested my hand on the phone and leaned against the wall. Carol had been my dearest friend in college, an anchor during my blindness. Already, in the past year, a month or two had passed between our phone conversations. Her marriage would mean even less contact. As yet I had no friend nearly as close, and I felt as if I had lost a limb.

Probably there were other reasons for the tears, equally self-pitying. Carol's life was moving on. I had forfeited a good relationship with Chuck and a good job at the guild. Now I didn't even have a course of study, and my health was falling apart again.

My nightmares about not making it alone were now real. I had no choice. I would have to give up all my hopes, all that I'd been striving for, and go back to my parents in Conyngham.

❧ 18 ❧

The next day, good old Gail Zimmerman called. "Hobart!"

My name, from her lips, always sounded like a command. Unconsciously, I whipped to attention.

"I have an idea for you," she said.

I braced myself.

"Talk to Ralph Peabody in Pitt's Department of Special Education. Maybe he could find a fellowship for you."

I made an appointment. Presto! One leftover government fellowship. I couldn't believe it. A reprieve. I wouldn't have to slink back to Conyngham just yet.

Not only did this fellowship pay tuition and books, it provided a monthly stipend, enough for me to live on without working. So I would be independent financially for the next eight months. Was my luck changing?

"We will try to snag you into special education," Dr. Peabody said. "Meanwhile, you can schedule as many counseling courses as we offer here, in case you still want the social work program. You could even earn credits toward that degree with some of our classes."

A week later, I received more good news. My second hearing test coincided exactly with the first. Maybe the fortune pendulum *was* swinging my way.

"Absolutely no change, Miss Hobart," said Dr. Stanziola, squeezing my wrist.

"I'm glad," I said, relaxing. "But I still want to find, well, pursue the cause. Doctors never found a reason for my blindness."

"I understand," he said. "And I'd like to schedule a battery of tests. But with this audiogram today, there is no rush. The holidays are approaching, and we can easily wait till January."

"All right," I said. January. This way the medical tests wouldn't interfere with final exams.

He stood. "If there is any change whatsoever, I want you to call me immediately."

I nodded. Two months ago I hadn't liked Dr. Stanziola, but he seemed less hurried during this appointment, more sensitive. And he'd given me good news. Good news for now, anyway.

❦ 19 ❧

I shivered all the way home from my nineteenth-century novels exam, and hauled open the front door of my apartment building. Done! No more finals for at least five months. And now vacation.

Standing in the lobby, I fumbled through my backpack for the mailbox key. Behind me, I heard the door open and felt a gust of biting wind.

"Sally, are you all right?"

I spun around, trying to identify the familiar voice.

"It's Dr. Stanziola," he said.

"My gosh. What are you doing here?"

"I was just parking the car for a luncheon meeting next door," he explained, "and saw you crossing the street. Are you all right? You looked uncertain, and I thought you might be dizzy again."

Wasn't that thoughtful! "No, I'm fine," I said, smiling. Sheepish. "Just wobbling from exhaustion. I stayed up all night studying."

"Shame on you," he said, touching my elbow. "Here. I'll help you to your apartment."

I shook my head. "No, thanks."

"Well, phone if you have any further trouble."

I pulled out the mail and clomped up the stairs, puffing as if carrying a heavy load. I was desperate for sleep, but needed to do laundry and pack.

My first impression of Dr. Stanziola had been completely wrong. What a considerate man! I tossed my coat and boots in the closet and yanked out my suitcase. Compassionate—that was what my minister would have called Dr. Stanziola. She'd preached on the subject last week: "Compassion—having love for ourselves and for all life."

I gathered up my dirty clothes and ran downstairs. The superintendent had allowed me to mark the dials of the machines in Braille.

An hour later, as I folded the warm laundry, the telephone rang.

"Sally, this is Dr. Stanziola."

I blinked. His name had come out thick and slow.

"Are you sure you're all right?" he asked.

His voice sounded different. Usually it cracked like thunder.

"I'm fine."

"I'd like to stop by and check on you."

The radiator clanged. Otherwise, silence. But alarms went off in my head. "That's not necessary, Dr. Stanziola."

"For my peace of mind, then." He cleared his throat. "I'd like to see you, Sally. You're very attractive—"

I hung up, shaking enough that the phone rattled in the cradle. I stopped holding my breath. Had I encouraged the man? Had I given off signals that I wanted this kind of attention?

I sat down and rummaged back through my mind to the office visits. I hadn't exuded enormous strength, but I hadn't fallen apart either. My behavior had been fine. I wasn't to blame for this phone call.

Compassionate? What a joke! The man was a predator, stalking the weak. How many other blind women—how many women, for that matter—had been exploited by men like this? I took out the anger on my suitcase, throwing shoes, boots, tapes, my folding cane into it.

How good to be going home for Christmas again, to be with my parents, my brother, my sister, her kids. Going home to clean, old, innocent Conyngham. After the phone call, I felt grimy, as if I'd swept a chimney.

I took a hot bath, ate, and went to bed. I lay in a haze between sleep and consciousness, listening for a knock, afraid that Dr. Stanziola would show up, claim rank.

In the morning I awoke to another phone call. I

reached for it, hesitated, then laughed at myself. The chances of a second unwanted call were slim.

"Sally, don't hang up."

Dr. Stanziola. I went stiff but, amazingly, obeyed his command.

"I owe you an apology. I'd had several cocktails yesterday—something I rarely do." He paused. "But there's no excuse for my behavior."

"No, there isn't," I agreed, icicle-cold.

"If you wish, I can refer you to another otologist."

I relaxed, ran my fingers through my hair. He'd apologized—I should give him credit for that. And getting oriented to a whole new doctor was so complicated.

I sighed. "This might be a mistake," I began, "but I'll allow one professional lapse. I want to be your patient—nothing more. I have enough problems. I do not want a relationship with a married man"—I hesitated—"old enough to be my father."

"I understand," he said.

Three hours later, I sat in the front seat of a Greyhound bus, its wheels carrying me closer to my old home. Farther away from turmoil.

Just before midnight I slid into the soft, comfortable slipper—home. I decided to say nothing about my problems with my ears or with Dr. Stanziola.

My second Christmas without any sight went more

smoothly than my first. I felt fewer longings to see the decorated tree, to see my nieces' and nephew's faces, how much they'd grown. Fewer longings to enjoy visual beauty.

Mom helped with something else that had overwhelmed me last year: shopping for Christmas presents. Shopping for anything was always an issue, a hassle. But this time the brood tagged along, Tracy insisting on holding my left arm, Erik my right, with Amy hanging on from behind. Not a mobility technique Gail Zimmerman would have recommended.

For two full weeks I relaxed and let Mom mother me. I didn't think about Dr. Stanziola or my hearing.

But 1970 and my vacation ended. The Greyhound returned me to Pittsburgh, to four new classes and, unfortunately, to new hearing problems.

In mid-January, my right ear blocked up, and I could barely hear with it. I sat in my apartment, stricken. I wouldn't go back to my parents. This wouldn't defeat me.

I snatched the telephone and placed it at my left ear, then paused. Should I really phone Dr. Stanziola? To find a new doctor, get a quick appointment, learn the route to his office—there wasn't time. And Dr. Stanziola was the expert on my condition.

I phoned. His receptionist scheduled an appointment for me that day.

I sat in the examining chair, my hands perspiring. I was as worried about facing the man as I was about the news he'd break.

The door opened. My heartbeat quickened. Cheek twitched.

"Hello," he said, swallowing the word, coughing.

The stool rolled beside me. Shaving lotion. Then his fingers on my earlobe, trembling. Nervous, like me.

"Sally, the audiogram shows a substantial change in that right ear."

Could it be wax? Plenty of people had wax build-ups, no matter how often they bathed.

He checked the left ear, sat back, and blew out a breath. "I'd like to put you in the hospital," he said.

Not wax. Something more serious. Always serious.

Twenty-four hours later, I entered Eye and Ear Hospital for tests. Emily, Ira, Ilene, Rachel visited. My minister came. She knew that I expected my hearing to go the way of my vision.

"You've said that when you were going blind, you prayed for both eyes, then for one, and finally for any amount of sight."

I nodded.

"But even though you didn't keep any sight, you found acceptance and peace."

Again I nodded, throat swelling.

"You prayed for a cure, Sally, and got a healing."

My mind opened to this new idea, filling me with comfort and relief. This Christmas had been better than last. Every week, every month, every year, there was more healing.

"If necessary, and the worst happened to your ears," she went on, "could you find that again?"

Maybe. But I began to pull back, tense, throw up defenses. Grateful as I was for the healing, this time I would beg with all my heart for the technical fix— the cure.

Mom flew out. "Your father and I will do whatever it takes to make you come home," she said. "The medical center in Danville is within a half hour, and New York City is—"

I held up my hand. "Please, Mom, please. Not now. Let's just get through these tests," I said. "I can't make any decisions now."

"I know," she said, hugging me. "I'm sorry. Sorry."

I gave a sigh. My hearing just had to stabilize. Then, somehow, I would persuade her to give me seven more months, until my fellowship ran out.

Together we made a list of all the urgent questions and held it until the last day, when every test would be finished. I wanted to remain calm.

Unfortunately, when Dr. Stanziola came to discharge me, Mom hadn't made it to the hospital yet. I had to pose the questions without her support.

"What kind of hearing loss do I have?"

"A nerve loss," he answered. "Not a conductive one."

"Can it be helped by a hearing aid?"

"No. Sorry."

"But what could be causing it?" Careful—voice rising.

"We don't know yet," he admitted, standing. Restless.

A week of tests, and he didn't know. A year of tests, and the eye doctors hadn't known. Why did I have to be so complicated?

I gripped the bed rail. "Are there more tests you'd like to do? Other doctors I should see?" Desperation. But I didn't care.

"Sweetie," he said, touching my leg. I snapped it away. "It's not that big a loss. You're just upset about this because you're blind." He chucked me under the chin. "I'll see you in two weeks." His footsteps disappeared through the doorway and down the hall.

My cheeks flamed. Not that big? Not now, but how big would it be in a year?

And wasn't being blind a good reason to be upset? I'd spent two years losing my sight while many doctors reassured me, "We'll stop this. We'll get to the bottom of this." Wasn't the old terror understandable?

And he'd cut me off before I'd asked all my questions. Three years ago I could have run down the hall and tackled him till he'd answered every one. But now . . .

I hurled my pillow toward the empty doorway.

Two days after I left the hospital, Dr. Stanziola called again, asking to come to my apartment. His voice turned my stomach. I slammed down the phone so hard I nearly dismantled it. I searched that day until I found a new doctor, Sidney Busis, even more respected than Dr. Stanziola.

But Dr. Stanziola was as persistent as a mosquito. Two weeks later he phoned again.

"You missed your follow-up appointment, Sally," he said, not bothering to identify himself.

Finally I decided to blast him. "Don't ever call here again," I said. "You're just lucky I haven't exposed you to the whole medical community."

Maybe I should have exposed him. But I was so tied up with concerns about my hearing, my courses, with just trying to lead an independent life in Pittsburgh, I didn't have any fight left over.

Still, I kept wondering why a man like that would think I'd be interested. Did some men assume that blind women would settle for anyone?

"Don't compromise," Ken had told me.

Well, I wouldn't compromise. And I didn't need to put up with hassles from any man. No blind woman needed to.

❦ 20 ❦

The special education courses and new books provided a thrill of pleasure, lifting me out of my problems. I attended classes, studied, and put Dr. Stanziola behind me.

One day in late February, I approached the Cathedral of Learning, summoning courage to walk through the revolving doors. My mind focused on entering and exiting with each finger intact.

I waited, hoping the swish, swish of the doors would quiet. Silence. My moment. I charged in and pushed, listening, feeling for the opening. Ha! There it was! I sprang ahead, once again the vanquisher.

"God, you're gorgeous," a woman cried, grabbing my wrist. "You look Jewish, except you're too tall."

The woman's voice was familiar, but I couldn't place it.

She laughed and swung my arm out to the side. "Will you look at her, Audrey? Couldn't you just die?"

I blinked and scrambled to regroup.

The woman took my hand. "I'm Sherry Broad, and this is Audrey Smith. We're in two of your classes."

"Hi," I managed to say.

"We're on our way to Dr. Peabody's class, too. Take Audrey's arm. She's studying to be a mobility instructor."

Audrey elbowed me. "Just salute and do whatever Sherry says." She laughed.

I obeyed, following along like a cocker spaniel. In the classroom, I took a seat between the two of them.

Dr. Peabody began his lecture. "Blindness separates you from objects. Deafness separates you from people."

I thought about this. Life without visible objects was bearable; life without people would not be. But for over a month now my hearing had been stable, and the dizziness had not returned. If my hearing never got worse, I could be perfectly happy. What remained was sufficient for all my needs.

Suddenly I realized that Dr. Peabody had stopped talking. In the front of the room I heard rustling, many footsteps, the sound of wood upon wood, chairs moving along the floor. What was going on?

"For the remainder of our time this afternoon," Dr.

Peabody said, "I've invited a panel of blind people to speak. From left to right, they are Kim, Loretta, Nan, and Virginia. Now, Sally . . ."

My back straightened.

"Feel free to pipe in at any time. The rest of you, ask anything that comes to mind."

Dr. Peabody's shoes clomped to the left of the room. "Panel, here is your opportunity. All these students, except Sally, are sighted. All will be teaching the blind."

Not all. I still planned to go into counseling.

"What would you most like to tell them?" finished Dr. Peabody.

There was a pause, but then the first person on the panel spoke up. Kim.

"Blind people are a varied breed," she began in a crisp soprano. "We are not all militants."

"I don't understand," said a man from the front of the class. "Can she explain?"

"*She* can explain," Kim snapped.

And I understood the sarcasm. I hated when people spoke to a sighted person with me instead of to me directly.

Kim went on. "I'm referring to those blind people who refuse to stow their canes on airplanes, for example. They are so independent they become a nuisance." She laughed. "Airlines are accommodating. The burden is on us blind people to adapt."

How would they get to the bathroom without their canes? They'd have to take the flight attendant's arm.

"I'm for us blind people doing the adapting," said another woman on the panel. Her voice was loud, conspicuous. Nan. "But I respect those militants. One of my blind friends wouldn't take a seat on a bus. He wanted to stand. Standing has nothing to do with vision," she explained, "just balance. Still, the bus driver pulled off the road and called headquarters for another bus. All the passengers had to move to that bus because the driver wouldn't go on till the blind guy sat."

Kim hit the table. "You're in favor of inconveniencing all those passengers?"

"Yup!" said Nan. "Trouble is, I don't have the guts." She gave an uproarious laugh. "But all of us blind people benefit from that guy's fighting discrimination."

"How is that discrimination?" asked Kim.

Sparks might fly any minute, but I was getting a kick out of the exchange.

"Sighted people thinking they know better what's good for us," she explained. "We can't see, so we must not be able to think. And we have to be protected. I know a blind minister who wants a big, urban church. But no, he was given a small, safe, rural one."

Ken had talked about this kind of "benevolent discrimination" in jobs, in housing. My thoughts strayed to my former student Scott, an automobile salesman before his blindness. He'd stopped writing, but still phoned now and then, usually when he'd had too much alcohol. He'd had hopes of other jobs, but had to operate a vending stand instead.

Dr. Peabody's watch or cuff link dinged on something metal—a chair, probably. "What about the rest of you, panel?" he asked. "Is there some burning issue you'd like to address?"

Nan laughed. "Sure is," she said. "I went to regular school, not a school for the blind. Well, I got royally teased! Food shot at me during lunch, the works. It was miserable."

Her voice sounded husky. The pain seemed as strong now as it had been years ago. Maybe all her laughter muffled the hurt.

"I went to regular school, too," added Kim. "When the teacher wasn't looking, the kids put their fingers over the end of the line of Braille I was reading so I couldn't finish the sentence. They pulled my hair."

"Maybe, as teachers, you could prepare the blind kids," continued Nan with warmth, "and try to make the sighted kids more accepting."

Could a teacher do that? I hoped so. By becoming blind in adulthood, I'd escaped ridicule, at least ridicule to my face.

131

Sherry called out, "Loretta, where did you go to school?"

"The School for Blind Children," she answered, "here in Pittsburgh."

"Do you think it was better there?" asked Sherry.

Loretta paused. "Well, I didn't get the teasing there," she said. "But I always wondered if I would have had a more normal social life in regular school, like my sister—dates, the teen things." She coughed. "I definitely didn't have the boyfriends."

Boyfriends. Ah, the "daily quest." I was twenty-seven now and having casual dates, nothing more.

"Plenty of us sighted women are without boyfriends," offered Audrey from behind me.

"Right!" cried Kim. "All the complaints about not having this or that because of our blindness—well, that stuff just rolls off my back. I'm blind. Big deal. I also have brown hair."

Without meaning to, I blurted out, "Are you suggesting that blindness is nothing more than an attribute like hair color?"

"Exactly."

"Is that your view, Sally?" asked Dr. Peabody.

I shook my head. "To me, it's a deprivation. And I can't change it the way I can change hair color."

"How old were you, Sally, when you went blind?" asked Dr. Peabody.

"Twenty-six when I lost everything," I said. "Twenty-four when it began."

"Maybe that's the difference," said Kim. "Blindness is the only way of life I've known. It's like having a million dollars. If you lose it, you have to change your whole way of life. If you've never had the money, you don't know what you're missing."

At the guild I'd heard that the congenitally blind feel their difference from others. The blinded feel the difference plus the loss.

"Virginia," Dr. Peabody said, "you've just become blind. Do you feel the way Sally does or the way Kim does?"

There was a long pause. "Sally," she said softly. "But I can't even think about the psychological stuff right now. I'm too overwhelmed just trying to cope with my son and my house."

The room hushed. "Could you explain?" Dr. Peabody's voice was gentle.

"My husband left several years ago. My son is six. And he's so angry that I can't play baseball with him, take him to the park easily. He's throwing tantrums, wetting the bed . . ." Her voice wavered. "And I don't have my house organized. My mom keeps saying that I went through this training, so I should have everything together, but . . ."

Her words were dry, weary. My heart went out to

her. How terrible to have so many pressures and responsibilities! If there was a good time to go blind, I'd found it. I'd had the luxury to grieve, to organize myself, to adjust without people counting on me.

Loretta spoke up. "Well, I was born blind, and I still feel that I've missed something. It doesn't take long to realize how much harder my life is. Sighted people can run here and run there. It's so easy. I definitely feel a loss."

At the guild they spoke of blindness as a kind of death. No one had suggested that the congenitally blind felt this death. But maybe they did.

Loretta continued. "We don't do as well socially, occupationally. Blind teens don't get part-time jobs. Few have chores, responsibilities."

"Well, I don't miss sight any more than I miss walking on the moon," said Kim. "The only reasons I'd want to see are to drive and read the newspaper."

Wow! I was adjusted to being blind, to never seeing again. But if Kim knew the many conveniences and pleasures of vision, she'd have more than two reasons for wanting to see.

"I already got driving out of my system," Loretta said. "I drove along Carson Street in the South Side."

"You what?" exclaimed Dr. Peabody, hitting a table.

Loretta chuckled. "My brothers and sisters told me to turn left, right, or brake."

"I drove in the snow," said Kim.

The entire class erupted in laughter.

Dr. Peabody stood. "Isn't this reassuring now as we go to our cars?" He laughed again. "Let's give a round of applause to our panel for an honest, thought-provoking session."

I stood. I hadn't heard this kind of discussion since I'd been a trainee. I missed it. Ken and I had always talked about living with blindness.

I began to walk out. I was so glad I'd found this fellowship. The panel's comments gave order to my experience. Even if I didn't teach the blind again, I was still learning, still shedding the dead husk of my old self for this new one, finding a new life.

⤙ 21 ⤚

"Sal, hang on," Sherry called from across the room. "I'll be there as soon as I ask Kim a question."

I smiled, remembering my experience with Sherry just two hours ago.

"You think Kim can handle an encounter with Sherry?" asked Audrey.

"An assault, you mean." I laughed. "Kim seems pretty tough."

"Right," agreed Audrey. "Tell Sherry I had to run along. See you on Thursday, Sal."

Sal? I smiled at the informality, then walked back a few steps to eavesdrop on Sherry and Kim's conversation.

"I think there are advantages to being blind," Kim was saying. "I have a voice. People think I have something important to talk about. I get attention, respect, praise."

I'd never thought about these things.

"And it generally brings out the best in people," she added.

Not always. I still reeled from the stories of teasing that she and Nan had told us.

"Do you agree with her?" Sherry asked as we walked down the hall.

"With some things," I said.

"Well, do you think there are advantages?"

My feet and cane went out of sync. I reached for her arm and let her guide me.

"The blindness changed me—made me stronger, more sensitive. Maybe more aware. I wouldn't want to give up these things, but I'd easily give up being blind."

We entered the elevator. When we left, I added, "I don't pity myself or want pity. Still, the blindness was mostly a tragedy, not a blessing."

We walked along the dank corridor.

"You have time for a cup of tea?" asked Sherry.

I nodded. "I have another class in half an hour, but tea would be great."

Sherry turned out to be five feet tall in shoes, but her presence was formidable. I couldn't resist her complete openness, quick intimacy. We exchanged phone numbers, and I snaked through the building to my counseling class.

The instructor, Dr. Seligman, reviewed basic counseling techniques, which I understood. As usual, we paired up, one of us pretending to be the counselor, the other pretending to be the client. In this way we practiced the techniques.

Next Dr. Seligman talked about nonverbal communication from the client, such as facial expression, eye contact, posture, and grooming. These things often communicated as much as what the client said.

I grew worried. Children, even the gabbiest, would clam up when talking about their problems. And, in addition, I had a hearing loss. Now I realized I would miss all the nonverbal cues, as well.

After class I detained Dr. Seligman. "Maybe I should give up the dream of working with kids, and work with adults."

"Why is that?" he asked.

"Well, how can I help depressed or angry kids when I can't see their nonverbal cues?"

He snapped his briefcase. "You can use your blindness to advantage."

Blindness an advantage. I warmed to the coincidence of this issue coming up twice in one day. Blindness—not a blessing, but not necessarily a curse.

"Explain to the kid that you cannot see how he is feeling," continued Dr. Seligman. "So he has to put his feelings into words." He sat on the desktop. "In time you'll perfect your listening skills to pick up more than just kicking of the foot, tapping of fingers. Some kids at first might be uncomfortable with your blindness, but many might feel more comfortable. You see the inner person. Teenagers with body-image difficulties will appreciate you."

I left the classroom, relieved. Maybe I could work with children after all.

Teenagers with body-image difficulties . . . This comment reminded me of something a recent date had said. "Lucky for me you can't see, or you probably wouldn't go out with me." He'd laughed. "At least that's what my buddies say."

I hadn't known how to respond. Sometimes people measure their self-worth by the appearance of the persons they date. Fortunately, I'd grown out of that years before.

That man and other dates blurred together—kind, good people, without expectation or demand.

Graduate school was my main concern. Through the snow, ice, wind, and cold I struggled back and forth to class.

Finally, winter gave out, and spring arrived with its sweet, undefinable fragrances.

Sherry and I spent more and more time together. I asked her to update my wardrobe, and she shopped with me, making me once again snappy and stylish. We traveled to Conyngham and New York City. We attended movies, concerts, and the opera. Someone even slapped her leg to quiet her as she described a scene in *La Bohème* to me.

Over these months I'd grown to appreciate her great fund of loyalty and love. As our friendship deepened, I realized that I had finally found the friend I'd been seeking. Another Carol.

My grant ran out at the end of August. After taking four courses in the field, I was sure that counseling children was the career that would most satisfy me. I put together grants from the state and two Lions Clubs to finance the social work program. I couldn't wait to resume my studies in the fall semester.

Instead of visiting my parents during my week's vacation, I traveled to Cape Cod, Massachusetts, where my friend Rachel and her family owned property. Twice I had spent summers waitressing on the Atlantic coast, once on Nantucket Island, Massachusetts, and another time at Bar Harbor, Maine. But I hadn't been to the Atlantic since becoming blind.

I stood knee-deep in the bay, marveling. The ocean, ancient, majestic, gave pleasure to every sense, not just sight. Rushing wind, pounding waves, birdcalls, sand, warm on top, cool, damp underneath—all were delights.

I still could enjoy travel, even to places of great visual beauty. And nothing about being blind kept me from enjoying the water. Twice in my teens I'd tried waterskiing, without luck. I'd seen the boat speed ahead, the rope tighten, and had pulled myself up only to pitch forward into the water. Now I tried it again.

Rachel was driving the boat. "If I hit the rope three times, Sally, you know to let go," she said. "Either there's too much traffic or there's something in your way."

"Like a dock," I called, laughing, bobbing in an open-cannonball position.

"Here we go," yelled Rachel.

Crouched, knees to chest, skis pointing in, I felt the roaring boat yank the rope forward. Trusting only to feel, I sensed the water beneath my skis, mushy, then hard as a tabletop. I stood. Once again, blindness worked to advantage.

I charged across the water, waves spraying, knocking me, making me wobble, rope dipping, but always towing me, stretching my arm and shoulder muscles. Wild wind. Ocean salt on my lips. Eyes open. Nothing but sunlight. Brilliant. Gleaming. I zoomed through the one thing I could still see—the dazzling, wonderful sunlight. I wanted it to last forever.

⚮22⚮

My two years of graduate studies seemed uneventful, with a few exceptions. The first was another hearing blockage in the fall semester, 1971. More tests. More doctors. More anguish. A four-month blur.

But in the end, no more hearing loss. From January 1972 my hearing remained stable, and I moved forward, learning more counseling techniques, approaches, theories, diagnoses. I spent fifteen hours a week in field placements, first at the Allegheny East Mental Health–Mental Retardation Center, then, in September 1972, at Western Psychiatric Institute and Clinic. In both places I worked with a variety of people: teenagers, parents, guidance counselors, the mentally retarded.

With each new client, I concentrated first on making a perfect landing from the waiting room to the office. Smooth as an eel I maneuvered, without bumping anything, without entering the wrong office, without sitting on the floor instead of my desk chair. All competence, confidence. Usually, by the time the client had taken his seat, he'd stopped worrying about me and settled down to his own concerns.

All the work was critical to my training, but one experience stood out. While at Western Psychiatric, I asked to work four hours a week at the nearby School for Blind Children. My clients were college-bound seniors, terrified at facing the sighted world. Since I'd spent the past three years practicing that very task—facing the sighted world—I was eager to help.

First they asked basic questions about obtaining college books on tape or in Braille, about finding their way from dormitories to classes. By the second week their questions shifted to the scarier stuff: interaction with those unknown beings, sighted students.

I gave them the typical advice for finding friends: join clubs, participate in campus activities. But their worries stemmed from more obvious issues related to their blindness.

"Back home, kids teased me about my clothes," one girl offered.

"Since I became blind, my brother says I don't hold up my head," said a boy next to me.

"My cousin is always exercising and dieting," another girl said. "She thinks I should lose weight, too."

Appearance *would* be a factor in their acceptance by sighted students. I brought in Sherry with most of her wardrobe, plus her brother's and mine. "Try this on," she said to one student after another.

The kids had a ball learning about fashions, complementary colors, hairstyles. We suggested that in the future they speak to employees at hair salons and clothing stores for reliable feedback.

Sherry helped me teach hand gestures, facing people, shrugging the shoulders, nodding or shaking the head. "When these things are missing, sighted people might make the unconscious decision that you're different from them," I said, "that you have nothing in common."

Christmas vacation, 1972, marked the end of my work at the School for the Blind and brought a surprise letter to my mailbox—from Maria, my first California roommate. Enclosed with the letter was a round-trip plane ticket to California funded by the teachers in my former district. At first I hesitated to accept the generosity, but Sherry and my other friends persuaded me to go. I canceled my plans to go to Conyngham.

Four days later I flew out, remembering my last tormented flight to and from California, to decide whether or not Tom and I should marry. I sighed, then smiled. The past came back like indigestion!

Maria met me at the gate with old "Lone Egg" Brian. We hadn't gotten together for three years. Maria and her first husband had divorced, and she and Brian were clearly in love. Compared to Brian and Maria, my dates of the last two years and I were plodding mules, companiable, nothing more. And at twenty-nine I felt old age creeping up on me. Would I ever fall in love again?

Mrs. Howell, the mother of one of my former third graders, arranged a party. More than a dozen kids, all middle-schoolers now, poured in, cool and gusty as a cold front. They'd perfected the appropriate teenage posturing. But a few of the girls set aside their learned behavior and rushed up with enthusiastic hugs. The boys hung back, their comments carefully chosen.

But soon they all warmed up, and I sat among them while time collapsed. I was their same Miss Hobart —except that I couldn't see now. As I spanned two lifetimes, I felt the enormity of the change bear down on me.

Mrs. Howell gathered us into a circle around a tape recorder. Each student recalled favorite memories of our third-grade class—our newspaper, flutophone concert, letters to American soldiers in South Vietnam, reading of *Pippi Longstocking*, "Mr. and Mrs. Clean" weekly desk awards. I fought tears. Tears for a colossally easier life, gone forever. For a cherished profession, lost. For the wonder of kids.

I returned to Pittsburgh, home, and closed the book on my California life. I was aware of many blessings. My health was holding up, my career was developing, and I had beautiful friends, old and new. No love, but I wasn't bereft. In fact, for the first time in five years, I felt complete again, restored.

Early in the new year, 1973, I met Emily Feldstein at the Craig Street Inn. After a while, Jimmy, the bartender, joined us on his break, taking the seat next to me. Just then Emily's husband and his new friend, Adam, arrived. They talked with us briefly, then left.

A minute later, Adam returned. "Sally, I thought you were with him!" he exclaimed, meaning the bartender.

Adam asked me to dance, and I learned that he was a tree trunk of a man, smelling of coffee and peppermint candy.

"I love your perfume," he said, "your neck." He kissed my hair.

Midway through the song, he leaned back and said abruptly, "I'm going to treat you like any other girl."

Those few, candid words a revelation, explaining years of kind, unexciting dates. The other men had been overgentle—maybe afraid to hurt someone who was already injured. I valued gentleness, especially in a man. But I missed the vigor and lustiness of the men I'd known in my sighted life, men like Adam.

Adam was an open, sweet guy with the voice and manner of a machine gun. Totally unmonogamous. We dated very briefly, but he would remain special. He'd identified what I was missing in relationships. He reminded me what I was holding out for, and he paved the way for another full-blooded man, who came along three months later.

23

"Come on in," I told Bob, squeezing his hand. Firm. Large. He'd just arrived for our first date.

One of my readers had fixed us up, sure that we'd like each other. The date actually had been scheduled for the night before, but Bob had phoned, asking to postpone it a day. He'd been invited to a party and wanted to attend, obviously without the encumbrance of a date. Though annoyed, I'd agreed, exposing my empty calendar.

"Would you like something to drink?" I smiled up at him. Tall. Probably over six feet.

"What are you serving?" he asked.

The location of his voice dropped, and I realized he was leaning on the bookshelf that doubled as a kitchen counter.

I trailed my fingers along the shelf, then rummaged through the refrigerator. "Only scotch, I'm afraid, or Tab. Sorry."

"No problem," he said easily. "I'll take that."

I cocked my head. "But which one?"

"Scotch and Tab," he said, as if that were the most common drink in any bartending book.

I fumbled for a glass. In Conyngham, in my family especially, men drank alcohol with water, plain soda, or ice. Women concealed the alcohol with Coke or other soft drinks. But not even a woman would drink the bizarre combination of scotch and Tab. I smiled to myself.

I took a Tab, and we sat down.

"How was the party last night?" I asked, hoping the question didn't have an edge.

"Great," he said. "My students had asked me to go—an international festival at the college. Food, dress, music, dance—all from different countries, all organized by the Point Park international kids."

I would have enjoyed that party.

"I thought about inviting you," he continued, "but I knew it would be a mob scene. I thought it'd be nicer like this."

Nicer? Well, I did hate enormous parties. I still hadn't forgotten the dreadful evening with Ted.

Outside the apartment, we hopped a cab. No car, I surmised.

"Hope you don't mind the cab," he said.

This man was reading my thoughts.

"I only own a bicycle and have no need for a car."

I smiled. "This is fine," I said.

Conyngham men craved a car from the time they were in a playpen. To be out of graduate school and have a job, yet no car—this, too, by Hobart standards was unusual. But then, who needed a car in the middle of Pittsburgh?

As we entered the theater, I wondered why I was worrying about this man fitting into Conyngham, into my family. This was only our first date.

I concentrated instead on the muscle in the arm that I held. He must lift weights.

Bob bought us candy and guided me to the left-hand side of the theater along an empty aisle. I heard no throats clear, no bodies rustle anywhere around me.

"I'll have to narrate some of the movie," he said, "so I picked an empty spot. I don't want to disturb anyone and take a blow on my already oversized nose."

I laughed. He could joke about himself. Score one. And no other date had thought of narrating to me. Score two.

Bob had described buildings or scenes out the cab window in a relaxed, interested way, not in an effort to fill holes in the conversation. Words came easily from him—not surprisingly, since he was an English professor. And I warmed to the words, remembering the frustrating, cool muteness of Tom.

When the movie began, Bob slid his arm around me, a move so natural that I hardly noticed. He began to detail the opening scenes of *The Way We Were*. Soon I identified Barbra Streisand's and Robert Redford's voices, other characters', too. After the first ten minutes, I was engrossed and able to keep up with the plot. Only once in a while did I feel lost, and Bob filled me in without my asking.

As I chewed a Good & Plenty, I remembered Chuck's tactics for keeping me awake in films—jabs, tickles, never narration.

The Way We Were was not an outstanding movie, but it had many romantic scenes for Bob to describe. That certainly accelerated our relationship.

When we returned to my apartment, I asked if I could get Bob anything.

"I'll have the usual," he said.

Scotch and Tab. That was my first experience of the man's dry sense of humor.

I sliced cheese and put it on a plate with crackers. Somehow we strayed to the subject of the Middle East.

"Israel is like a bumblebee," he said. "I've heard somewhere that by the laws of aerodynamics it shouldn't fly, and yet it does."

I smiled at the image.

"I'm Jewish," Bob said, "but I still think the Israelis have to sacrifice some land for peace."

For an hour we talked. Bob spoke energetically and with feeling on all sorts of topics.

Then the phone rang.

"So is this one Mr. Knightley?" the caller asked.

"Hi, Sherry," I said.

I had told her that I was holding out for a man like Mr. Knightley, the hero of Jane Austen's *Emma*.

"Could be," I said, smiling. "May I call you back?"

"He's still there?" she demanded.

"Yes." I hung up.

Bob noticed the time then and stood. He paused at the door and gave me a kiss—not a quick one either.

Mustache. Soft. Nice mouth. And glasses. I smiled. The nose *was* oversized.

"Are you free Thursday night?" he asked.

I nodded, then listened while he walked down the hall.

When Bob's footsteps disappeared, I telephoned Sherry.

"So?" That was how she answered. Not even a hello.

I just laughed.

"Well, what did you think?"

"He's different," I said, "but I like him."

Not the most flattering assessment, but still positive. I did like him. Bob was direct and open and interesting. And full of the vital ingredient, vigor.

"Are you going out with him again?" Sherry asked.

"On Thursday night," I said.

"Not for four whole days?" she exclaimed, obviously disappointed. Implying that sparks hadn't erupted.

"Right. He's finishing up his dissertation and teaching four classes. He has a full life."

And I had demands myself. I was winding up graduate school, taking finals, and facing joblessness once again.

During March and April 1973 I'd been offered four jobs, all at Western Psychiatric. However, President Richard Nixon's recent wage and hiring freeze had made those job offers collapse like dominoes. Without work, my hopes of staying in Pittsburgh would collapse, too.

But despite my job search and Bob's work, we went out together three and four times a week. Sunny patches amid the fog.

Sherry kept pressing me about my feelings for Bob, but I could only laugh and shake my head. I was happy when I was with him, happier than I'd been with anybody else. To explain further was as impossible as holding a beam of light. I knew I was growing to like him a lot, maybe too much, and I thought he liked me. But could I really count on him? Without meaning to, I soon put him to that test.

⚡ 24 ⚡

"How will you get to work every day?" the staff psychologist asked at my job interview.

Before I could answer, Charlie, the head of the mental health center, laughed and broke in. "She got here today, didn't she?"

I smiled, grateful that he'd made light of the tough question. But I had expected it and had an answer. "A friend drove me today," I said. "If you hired me,

I would learn the bus route and take public transportation."

The interview was going well. I liked these people and the sound of the job they were trying to fill: child therapist. For weeks I had been pounding the streets, answering ads that did not interest me at all. This appointment was a refreshing change.

"How would you read the records and reports?" asked the staff psychiatrist, the last person present.

I had anticipated this question, too. "During my field placements I used my own readers," I explained. "My supervisors interviewed them and discussed the importance of confidentiality. I paid the readers and would expect to do that here."

Charlie spoke up then. "And I'm sure our secretaries could fill in some of the time."

I warmed to this man and wondered why he was so supportive. In previous interviews I'd heard many concerns about my ability to handle the job. Most of the questions had been valid. Why should they hire an unknown blind person, who might need special services and considerations, over a sighted applicant?

When the interview ended, Charlie guided me out. "My ex-wife's brother is blind," he explained.

I smiled. "That's why you're so matter-of-fact."

"Right," he said. "Did their questions upset you?"

I stopped. "No. I thought they were fair. Why?"

"At one point I thought I saw tears in your eyes," he said.

I brushed my fingers lightly over my right eye. "I don't know what's going on today. This eye keeps stinging and tearing." I frowned. "Anyway, I wasn't upset."

"Good," he said. "I'll be in touch."

I left the office, optimistic for the first time. Maybe I would have a job soon.

Back home, I placed a warm compress over my eye. It had begun to throb.

I hadn't yet been to an eye doctor in Pittsburgh, since I went to Dr. Taggart for checkups when I visited my parents. I did have the name of a local doctor, but I didn't call. Probably I was just tired. My parents had come to Pittsburgh the previous weekend, ostensibly to celebrate Daddy's birthday on June 6, but really to check out Bob. We'd stayed up late, and I still hadn't caught up on sleep.

I phoned Bob to cancel our dinner plans, then stretched out for a nap.

By morning the pain was more severe than any I'd ever felt. The eye was racked by a pulsing, diffused ache that stalled my movements, blocked my thinking.

I fumbled for the phone and called Dr. Taggart at his home nearly three hundred miles away.

"Sally." He spoke my name firmly, slowly. "Is anyone with you?"

I shook my head, then reeled from the pain.

"Answer me."

"No," I said. Even speaking hurt.

"You need to see a doctor. Go to an emergency room."

I nodded. More pain.

"Sally?"

"I'm here," I said, sliding down again on my bed. I was nauseous with pain.

"I'm calling your parents," he said.

"No!" I yelled. "Someone will take me."

I hung up and tried to think. The cab company. What was the stupid number? I dialed the first three digits and knocked the phone off the table. I swore.

I squatted, then sat beside the phone. With trembling fingers I dialed the number, gave my name and address, and lay down, exhausted from the effort.

The phone blasted, sending waves of sound through my head. I groped for it.

"The eye any better?"

Bob. He would help. I shook my head.

"Sal? Hey!"

"What?"

"What's wrong? Honey?"

Alarm sounded in his voice.

"Sally, can you hear me?"

I nodded. "Pain," I said.

"Don't move," he ordered. "I'll be right there."

Dial tone. "Hang up the phone," I whispered.

Something roused me. The intercom buzzed and buzzed again. I remembered the cab and sat up.

I made my way to the intercom. "Be right down," I said softly.

I slid into the clothes I was wearing the day before and grabbed my purse and sandals. I rinsed with mouthwash and stumbled out, holding the wall as I walked.

In the cab, I thought of Bob coming to the apartment. "Oh, no. He won't find me," I said.

"What?" asked the driver.

I lay across the backseat.

"Miss, you okay?" the driver called. "Miss?"

"Pain," I said.

At the Eye and Ear Hospital emergency room, the cab driver half carried me to a seat. I shoved some bills at him and thanked him, then leaned across the adjacent plastic chair. In this position I answered the nurse's questions. After an eternity, she helped me into an examining room, and I stretched out on the table. If only I could sleep, I'd escape the pain.

Different hands, different people checked my eyes. Hands moved me to a chair, moved my chin and forehead into a machine.

"My name is Dr. Lewis, Miss Hobart. Open wide," a voice said.

I wanted to cooperate. But the eye was raw, flaming.

Fingers held my eyelids open.

I blinked, groaned.

"Just a minute," said the voice. "Just trying to get pressure."

Finally hands pulled me back, and I rested my head.

"How long have you had glaucoma, Miss Hobart?"

Echoes. Bad news breaking. "How long have you been hard-of-hearing?" My head and eye, bursting.

"Miss Hobart?"

Glaucoma. What was left to go wrong?

"How long have you had glaucoma?" he repeated. Stern. Irritated.

"Probably twenty-four hours."

"What?"

"I don't know," I snapped. I waved my hand and took deep breaths. Some force was drawing my right eye down through my body, trying to make it touch my foot.

"Drink this Glyrol," someone said. "It'll relieve the pressure."

I drank.

"Who's your eye doctor here, Miss Hobart?"

"I don't have one," I managed to say.

But he must not have heard me. He repeated the question. More irritation. I wasn't doing this right. He was getting mad at me.

A name slid into my mind—the ophthalmologist I was supposed to connect with in Pittsburgh.

"Dr. Ingram," I said.

"Get Ingram on the phone," a man ordered.

I finished the liquid, then lay back in the chair. I'd never had pain like this. Constant. Insistent. If these doctors wanted to remove my head, I would agree.

I closed my eyes, breathed evenly, and waited for the aching to subside. How many of these chairs had I sat in over the past five and a half years? How many doctors had looked into my eyes, my ears?

Footsteps. Then a voice. "Dr. Ingram would like to speak to you. We filled him in on your condition."

I felt the telephone receiver and drew it to my ear. It was heavy and strangely cold. Smooth.

"Miss Hobart, I show no record of having seen you," the voice in the telephone said.

I nodded, swallowed, then pressed my temples with my free hand. "No," I said. Was the pain lessening?

"Miss Hobart?" he yelled from the phone.

I moved forward in the seat. My head didn't throb. "I never saw you," I said, thoughts clearing. "Dr. Charles Campbell in New York gave me your name. He did laser surgery—"

"I see," he interrupted, then paused. "The Glyrol you drank will relieve the pain temporarily. But for a permanent solution you have two choices."

His voice was impersonal, distant.

"We can shoot alcohol behind your eye or remove it."

Remove the eye. Just get rid of it like an unwanted hair under the chin or between the eyebrows. Pluck it with as little emotion as that. Leave a gaping hole in my skull. Oh, this doctor had feeling.

"Miss Hobart, are you there?"

"I'll consider your advice," I said into the receiver. Why not remove it? Nothing but a miracle would give it life again. Yet it would mean more hospitalization, more adjustment, another blow to my psyche, my physical integrity. And I wanted to start a new job.

"One thing more, Miss Hobart," Dr. Ingram said.

"Yes?" I sighed.

"You've undoubtedly lost your light perception in that eye."

I hadn't even noticed that. I closed my left eye and peered through the right. No light. No shadow. Just smoky white nothingness. I opened my left eye and saw light, sunshine, probably from a window. Gradations of light and shadow. I could not detect any of that with my right eye.

"I guess I have lost the light perception," I said flatly.

"I wouldn't count on getting that back," he said.

"No, I won't." I dangled the phone out for someone to take. It left my hand, and I dropped the hand to my lap.

Glaucoma. And the light perception was gone. More bad news. Always.

Remove the eye? I had to think. To talk to Dr. Taggart. To Bob.

I stood. "What does shooting alcohol behind the eye do?" I asked.

"Deadens the nerves to the brain, the pain nerves," Dr. Lewis said.

I swayed. "Essentially kills the eye, then?"

He took my arm. "Yes. Here are a few pills for you to take—Diamox. And here are prescriptions for more Diamox and for pain medication. You'll need to make a decision soon about the procedure you'd prefer. The pain will return."

I nodded. I would think. But now I just wanted to rest.

~≥ 25 ≥~

All the way home in the cab I refused to think. Later
I would call Dr. Taggart for his medical advice. But
right now I would go to bed.

At the apartment building I found Bob.

"I've been so worried," he said, holding me for a
long time.

Slowly I relaxed. A breeze blew against us, ruffling
my dress, my hair. A dry Santa Ana wind that had
crossed thousands of miles from California to Pennsylvania.

Bob biked to the drugstore for my prescriptions,
and I went inside to sleep. As soon as I unlocked the
apartment door, the telephone rang.

"Sally, this is Charlie," he said. "Can you start work
on Monday?"

"Wow!" I said, letting out a breath. "Monday."

I sank onto the bed. My thoughts whirled. The
glaucoma. Getting oriented to the buses, the office.

I couldn't ask for time to resolve this latest problem.
How would he know that I'd had two years of stable
health? He might offer the job to somebody else.

"Sure," I said.

I hung up and stretched out on the bed. What had I committed myself to? What would I do if the eye flared up on Monday morning? I'd be in no shape to walk, let alone work!

But I had no choice. I had to stop worrying now and rest. Then I could think what to do. Every cell in my body was tense. I inhaled enough air to deplete the room of oxygen and blew it out. Relax. Relax.

Remarkably, I did. I slept so soundly that I never heard Bob enter the apartment. I awoke only when I smelled the steaks sizzling and heard his low whistling.

"What happened to your classes this morning?" I asked.

"Hey, you're awake," he called. He came over and gave me a kiss. "Canceled them. No problem."

My throat tightened. Here was a good man.

That weekend I fully intended to phone Dr. Taggart. But I spent all Saturday and Sunday learning the bus routes to work and back. Monday morning I concentrated on memorizing the office with its maze of rooms. Charlie showed me the way to the grocery and drugstore because the ones near my apartment would be closed by the time I returned home from work. Then he taught me basic job procedures. By Tuesday I had clients, kids from eight years to sixteen—all either depressed or angry.

Two weeks slipped by. I loved the job, my kids, co-workers. The work seemed perfect for me.

During those two weeks my eye stung and teared. But the pain medicine made it bearable.

Not so in the third week on the job. The same racking, pulsing pain awakened me early Monday morning. As before, I phoned Dr. Taggart. He found me a bed at Scheie Eye Institute in Philadelphia.

Next I phoned Bob, but he must have been en route to work already. I called his office and left a message with his secretary. Then I phoned Charlie.

In a cab, I made my way to the airport, lying across the backseat. I couldn't bear the pain. The cabdriver and a skycap helped me buy the ticket, and somehow I managed to board the plane. Meanwhile, my parents covered the one-hundred-and-fifty-mile distance by car to the Philadelphia airport and met me.

Dr. Taggart arrived at the hospital soon after we did and dilated the eye with atropine drops. He measured the eye pressure. Every few minutes the nurses used more atropine. Within an hour the pain had subsided.

"Feel better?" Dr. Taggart asked.

I nodded.

"We need to check you thoroughly," he said, "but if it's strictly the glaucoma, these drops are all you'll need."

"How's that?" Daddy asked.

"This treatment works only when the eye is already blind," Dr. Taggart explained. "Otherwise, the high pressure would destroy the sight." He turned to me. "This way you don't need an operation—just the drops."

"Really?" I asked. "So no removing the eye, no alcohol behind it?"

"Right," he said, and paused. "This alternative is Conyngham treatment."

I smiled. So he had invented it, way back in the boonies of northeast Pennsylvania. That was why no one in Pittsburgh had suggested it.

"Have you published this in a medical journal, Webster?" Mom asked.

Dr. Taggart laughed. "No, Katie. Too busy fishing."

Someone came in then.

"Well," Daddy cried, "look who's here."

I felt a quick kiss. Mustache. Squeeze on my hand. Bob. Surprising me completely. He must have caught the next flight out of Pittsburgh after mine.

My eyes filled. Tom had had trouble coming to the hospital when it was less than an hour away. Bob came the three-hundred-mile distance seemingly without a second thought.

"Webster," Mom said, "this is Bob Alexander."

I heard Daddy stand and thump Bob on the back. "She's going to be okay, Professor," he said.

And I was.

I missed only three days of work that week and never took off another until Bob's and my wedding a year later, in June 1974. By then the glaucoma had worn itself out in my right eye. It never developed in the left, although slowly the light perception disappeared in that eye, too.

On our honeymoon, Bob and I toured England for a week and Ireland for two. As we strolled along the beach of the Dingle peninsula one drizzly afternoon, Bob picked up something from a tide pool and placed it in my hands.

I ran my fingers over it and felt a starfish, missing an arm. It wasn't scratchy, as I would have expected, but soft and spiny.

"It's still alive, I think." I remembered that a starfish could regenerate new life from only a portion of itself. I walked with Bob toward the breaking waves, bent, and placed it in the water. I wanted it to find new life, to grow whole again—as I had.

Then I turned to Bob. "Let's hit a pub for tea," I suggested.

"Are you cold?" he asked.

"No," I said, linking my arm through his. I grinned and kissed him. "Not a bit."